theme games 2
Great games to help 7-11s explore the Bible

Lesley Pinchbeck

Scripture Union, 207-209 Queensway, Bletchley, MK2 2EB, England
www.scriptureunion.org.uk

ISBN 1 85999 590 X

British Library Cataloguing-in-Publication Data. A catalogue record for
this book is available from the British Library.

Cover design: PRE design consultants

Illustrations: Neil Pinchbeck

Printed in Great Britain by Creative Print and Design (Wales), Ebbw Vale

♨ Scripture Union is an international Christian charity working with
churches in more than 130 countries providing resources to bring the good
news about Jesus Christ to children, young people and famillies – and to
encourage them to develop spiritually through the Bible and prayer.

As well as our network of volunteers, staff and associates who run holidays,
church-based events and school Christian groups, we produce a wide range
of publications and support those who use our resources through training
programmes.

Contents

FOREWORD

If you've used the original *Theme Games* book, you'll need no
introduction to *Theme Games 2*! Here are even more ways of livening
up your mid-week clubs and Sunday groups with a whole new book of
over 80 theme-linked games.

Plus a comprehensive Bible index with over 200 references to the most-
used texts to help you link up with the right game.

And a theme index with over 120 headings to choose from!

Children and adults alike will have fun discovering the Christian
message together through games.

If you are new to *Theme Games*, read on for a comprehensive 'How to
use' introduction...

Have fun!

Lesley Pinchbeck

INTRODUCTION

Why 'theme games'?

Playing games with children can be much more than just a 'fun time' in a programme of youth work. This book aims to show how the ideas which we try to communicate through Bible study and other teaching materials can be brought to life through games.

Lots of the available teaching material for use with children relies heavily on a high degree of literacy in order to present ideas. We confront them, all too often, with a wall of words: 'Turn to page x', 'Read the story on page y', 'Look up these verses and answer the questions', and so on. Using games as a teaching aid is a simple, effective and fun way of lowering this literacy barrier, and of capturing the attention and interest of all children. Talking about a concept or reading about it can prove difficult for some children to grasp. Play a game about it with these children, however, and they will remember and experience the concept. They are then much closer to an understanding of what it means.

Games become learning experiences when children discover things for themselves in a real and tangible way. Playing a game makes them look at things around them in a new light, as they begin to experience the reality of what they have been hearing or reading of creation in Genesis. 'God made everything' ceases to be theory and becomes a visible fact.

All these games are intended to be supplementary to whatever teaching material is being used; find a game to liven up a rather solid session, or use the ideas here to make more of an already good programme. Add a new dimension to your fun and games.

What is a 'theme game'?

Many of the games in this book are simple variations of well-loved old favourites and old-fashioned party games. The latter are often surprisingly popular; in this hi-tech age, party games often seem quite novel to many children.

Whatever the game, or its origin, the importance is in the application – what you do with it – and the discussion and thinking time afterwards. If children can discover for themselves, through thinking about a game they have just played, what the theme of the day's session is to be, that information and the ideas arising are likely to remain fixed in their minds. This is much more effective than any announcement you may make on the matter – a case perhaps of actions speaking louder than words!

Using *Theme Games 2*

Each game is laid out in simple format, with a guide as to suitability for age groups, group sizes, playing space etc. If special equipment is needed, this is listed at the beginning.

The thematic index is based on the many common subjects in Christian Bible teaching, eg Armour of God, Commandments etc. A number of games can be adapted to fit almost any theme or subject matter.

At the end of each game description, the 'Theme points' section identifies the major theme and spells out exactly how to use the game to draw out from the group whatever point or theme you are trying to get across. Many games can be used to make several different points, eg there is overlap between hearing, listening and obeying. All these points are listed.

To help you in choosing your theme games, use this simple checklist of thinking points.

Think about...

1 ...what your theme is to be. This may be very obvious to you, but sometimes it can be difficult to decide exactly what is the main point of your study. There can be an overlap of several themes in one study. Try to see what it is that God is saying to you, today in that particular session – and stick with it. Too many theme points can be confusing.

2 ...when in the session you want to play a game/games. It is often useful to begin your meeting with a theme game. Games make good curtain raisers for any event; they break down barriers, help people relax, and draw the group together as they have fun through a common activity. When the starting point is also a theme game, you begin with the group already having established in their minds the direction you will now be taking with your Bible study. The session then begins with everyone that much more tuned in and receptive to the points which will then be raised.

A 'games break' during your session can provide a welcome relief for the more energetic and fidgety group members – and their leaders! If the game is also a theme game it means that continuity is kept – the topic is kept alive, and reinforced, by the game they play. You are then able to return to your study session with the group refreshed, and better able to concentrate, having released pent-up energy, and having gained a new slant on your theme.

3 ...what kind of game you will need to play. Indoors? Outdoors? Noisy? Quiet? Do you want to liven things up or calm them down? A lively game is sometimes usefully paired with a quieter game. The lively game provides the ice-breaking, warming-up time, and the quieter game helps players focus as you move into the rest of the session.

4 ...how many games you want to play. Playing more than one game with the same theme and then asking the children to identify the common idea that links them can be a useful way of drawing the 'theme' idea from the group, rather than just telling them what it is.

5 ...where you will be playing the game. Some games are obviously best played outside on a fine day (eg water games) but most can be played in whatever space is available. Make sure you have a suitable playing space ready and waiting so that you can go straight into your game. If necessary be ready to organise everyone to stack chairs and clear a space, or to adjourn temporarily to a suitable playing area.

6 ...the ages of your players. Most of the games in this book work well with all children in the 7-11 age group. You will know your own group and be best placed to make the final decision, but games marked with the 7-9 logo (see page 11) are perhaps more suitable for the younger age group.

7 ...the feelings of the players. Some children may be reluctant to join in – never force anyone! The whole point of playing a theme game is that everyone should relax, enjoy the fun and see things for themselves. Reluctant games players often get drawn into things, in spite of themselves, when they see others having a good time. Even those stubborn characters who remain resolutely on the sidelines will get the point you are making simply by seeing and hearing all that is going on.

8 ...the players themselves. This may seem obvious but it can be easy, when planning a group session, to overlook aspects of some games which could cause problems for handicapped members. This does not necessarily mean that you completely exclude these games from your repertoire; but it does mean that you will need to be aware of potential difficulties and be prepared to think of ways round them. For example, a child with a hearing problem might find a listening game almost impossible. You could include the child in the game quite easily and without embarrassment – another important factor – by giving them a role to play (eg tape-recorder operator, score-keeper, quizmaster etc). The same thinking applies to physically handicapped children who may find very active games difficult. Try pairing them with a 'runner' or 'helper'; appoint them as 'referees' and 'linesmen'. The important thing is to work out in advance what part you will ask them to play. At all costs avoid the last-minute 'Oh dear! What about you?' situation, which helps no one.

9 ...numbers of players. How many will there be? Very small numbers can play most of the games. Even two teams of three work reasonably well. Don't forget to co-opt leaders to make up numbers and balance teams where necessary. Some games may be difficult with very large numbers and you may need to subdivide the group to play the game effectively.

10 ...teams. Some games have to be played in teams for the game to work: in others, teams provide a way of breaking a large group into manageable numbers. Be careful how this subdivision into teams comes about – best friends tend to stick together, which is not always helpful; there will inevitably be someone left out; the most able and agile members may all end up in one team, and so on! It is difficult to achieve a fair balance between teams every time, but there are ways of managing fair(er) play.

For two teams, the simplest device is probably just to number everyone off – '1, 2, 3, 4...' – and then announce that the teams are to be odds and evens. If you are really cunning you can allocate your numbers so that you achieve balance of abilities etc without the players realising it is happening.

Alternatively, and this is useful for splitting rivals or best friends constructively, pick two children and tell them to pick their team members in turn. Everyone gets picked eventually. If you use this method make sure everyone ultimately has a turn to be a team picker.

In a really large group where you will need three or more teams, you will need some kind of team identification (eg coloured team bands).

11 ...your leaders. You may be running the session single-handed – make sure the game you choose poses no problems if this is the case. If you have several leaders, make sure that all of those who are helping know what the game is about, what the rules are, and what the theme point of the day is. It may help you to jot down the game title and main points of the game on to a postcard beforehand for quick on-the-spot reference when your mind goes blank at a vital moment! This is particularly useful if you intend to play more than one game with the same theme.

12 ...reactions to the games. 'Theme points' for each game will give some guidance as to how to use each one sensitively and to make your point. Be alert, however, for group members who may have found your particular 'point' hard to handle. This is especially important in role-playing where emotions may run high. Give everyone the time and opportunity to talk out their feelings and return, emotionally, to the here and now. It is helpful to emphasise the fun aspect of this kind of game. Emphasis on this will help counteract frustration and aggression felt by some to whom winning is all-important.

13 ...competitiveness. There will always be some players for whom winning will be more important than the game itself. Be alert for these children and try to emphasise the fun aspect to them; don't let over-competitiveness from a few spoil the fun of the majority.
On a practical level:

a. If you reward winners (even verbally) then reward everyone else as well for taking part.

b. Never put down a loser – or losing team.

c. Include a variety of games so that different skills are brought to the fore. There is seldom one individual who is the fastest and the most agile and has the best general knowledge and memory etc. Use variety to help the group to appreciate each other's differing talents.

d. Whatever skills may be needed, always look for opportunities for the most able to help the less able.

14 ...what happens afterwards. At the end of your meeting it may be helpful to recap briefly on any game(s) played. Children who didn't quite see the point at the time may now be able to do so more readily. They may like the opportunity to play the game again if they particularly enjoyed it. Use your discretion here; it can be frustrating to be rushed through a game you are enjoying simply in order to get on with other things. Knowing there will be further opportunities to play for fun at the end could be a great help – and something to look forward to afterwards. You may prefer, of course, to reinforce your theme by playing another, different game as a finale.

15 ...equipment. None of the games call for any specialist or hard-to-obtain equipment. If equipment is required, this is always listed at the beginning of the game description. It is worth mentioning here that foam sponge tennis balls and footballs are much safer and easier to use in a group than the real thing. Beach balls and balloons can often be substituted for these to make it possible to play almost any ball game indoors. A ball made from (clean!) old socks turned inside out and stuffed with socks or tights – a stitch or two secures this nicely – also makes a cheap and cheerful substitute as a ball for an indoor game.

16 ...compiling your own collection of theme games. You may well have come across a game similar in application to those described here. If you played it, and it worked – save it!

Invent your own! Begin by praying for inspiration, then try to identify the key thoughts and actions involved in your session. Now think about how these could be applied or drawn out of the game. You may then be able to see how an existing game could be used. For example, if your theme is 'jealousy', play 'Pass the parcel' and discuss how the losers felt. Add it to your collection!

Key to logos

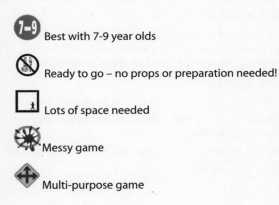

Best with 7-9 year olds

Ready to go – no props or preparation needed!

Lots of space needed

Messy game

Multi-purpose game

1 All change!

Themes

Easter, Christmas, Harvest, Pentecost, Bible heroes, emotions – use the game to fit your needs.

You will need

Pre-prepared list of session-related subjects, eg:

Easter – bunnies, chocolate, eggs, hot cross buns, chicks. (Talk afterwards about why these have come to be associated with Easter.)

Christmas – snowmen, holly, robins, presents, decorations, Santa. (Talk afterwards about why we have come to associate these with Christmas.)

Harvest – vegetable and fruit names

Pentecost – fire-related things: candle, matches, lightning, fireworks, bonfires. (Talk afterwards about the qualities of fire, and why the Holy Spirit took on the appearance of 'tongues of fire' at Pentecost.)

Emotions – fear, anger, jealousy, etc.

Noah – animals.

Fruit of the Spirit – love, joy, peace, patience, kindness, goodness, faithfulness, gentleness, self-control.

Bible Heroes – David, Moses, Paul, Joshua, Ruth, Elizabeth, Mary etc.

Adapt this game to your needs.

To play

Ask the children to form a large circle.

If there are only a small number of children, use only three or four words from your list. Name each child in turn after an object or word from your theme list. For example, with a Harvest theme and eight children playing, have two carrots, two cabbages, two parsnips and two onions. If you have a large group, then you can have more objects, and/or more children in each category.

Explain that you will be calling out words from your list in turn, at random. When you do so, all of the children in that category must run and change places with each other, as fast as possible.

When you call the buzzword (change this to fit your session), ALL children must run around and keep changing places until you call 'HOME!'

Everyone must stay in their new places for another round of changes. Buzzwords could be 'Harvest', 'Christmas' or simply 'All change!'

Theme points

Use this game to start discussions relevant to your chosen topic. You can also point out how everyone had to keep listening carefully. We have to keep our ears tuned to hear God speaking to us.

2 Animal antics

Themes

Creation, Noah

Bible link

Genesis 1; 6:9 – 9:17

You will need

Strip of paper per child (A4 cut in half lengthways is ideal), pens.

To play

Sit everyone in a circle, and give them each a piece of paper and a pen. Get them all to fold the paper in half, and in half again, so that they have four equally sized spaces from top to bottom of their paper strips.

Ask them all to think of an animal – any animal at all. In the top space, without letting anyone else see their drawing, everyone should draw the head of their chosen animal, ending with a neck on the first crease. Next, fold the top down so that only the ends of the neck are visible, and pass their paper to the child on the left. Continue to draw, first the bodies and then the legs, folding and passing the paper each time as before.

Finally, everyone must write the name of their chosen animal at the bottom of the paper strip. Pass to the left one more time, unroll, and have a good laugh at your impossible creatures!

Theme points

Talk about how wonderful and varied the animals that God has made are. For a Noah link, you can ask them to think of, and draw, animals that Noah took into the Ark.

3 Are you sleeping?

Themes

Jairus' daughter, Lazarus, fear

Bible link

Matthew 9:18–26; Mark 5:21–43; Luke 8:40–56; John 11:1–44

You will need

Clear playing space with defined limits, coat or small blanket.

To play

The whole group begin the game standing round in a circle, holding hands. Ask for a volunteer to be the first 'sleeper'. The sleeper goes to the centre of the circle and lies or crouches down with the coat or blanket over their head and shoulders, pretending to be asleep.

The rest of the players, holding hands, walk in a circle around the sleeper, and chant:

'One, two, three!
One, two, three!
Are you sleeping?
Can't catch ME!'

On the final shout of 'Me!', the sleeper must throw off the blanket, jump up, and run and tag one of the players. The first player to be tagged becomes the next sleeper in the middle. Players must stay within the playing space; make this as small or large as you wish, depending on how easy you want it to be for the sleeper to tag a player.

Theme points

How did you feel when the sleeper threw off the blanket and jumped up? Although you were expecting this to happen, it could still feel a bit scary as you walked round and waited for it.

How do you think people felt when Jairus's daughter got up, alive, when Jesus took her hand? Their first reaction was probably shock, but then they couldn't stop talking about what had happened.

How do you think Lazarus's family and friends felt when he came out of the tomb? It must have been a real shock as well, even frightening.

How do you think they felt when they realised that Lazarus was alive again? They wanted to tell everyone about what they'd seen.

4 Ark larks

Theme

Noah

Bible link

Genesis 6:9 – 8:19

You will need

Large container of water, junk – for example, egg boxes, bin bags, balloons, straws, sticky tape, Lego people and/or animals.

Top tip!

Make sure each team has the same pieces of junk.

To play

Put the children into small teams and give them each a selection of junk items to work with. They have ten minutes and within that time, their challenge is to build a floating ark that will carry two Lego people or animals. At the end of the time, try out all the arks in the water and award points for the most artistic, the most seaworthy etc.

Theme point

Use as an introduction to exploring the story of Noah and the flood or simply as an ice-breaker game.

5 Armour race

Theme

Armour of God, salvation

Bible link

Ephesians 6:10–18

You will need

One set of adult-sized clothing per team (one hat, one sweatshirt, one wide belt, pair of boots, coat/jacket), Bible, dice, easy-to-read labels, stuck onto the relevant garments: Hat = SALVATION, Belt = TRUTH, Sweatshirt = RIGHTEOUSNESS, Boots = GOOD NEWS (one word on each boot), Coat = FAITH, Bible = SWORD.

To play

Divide your group into teams of four or more, with one set of clothes per team. Give each team a dice, and tell them to choose a volunteer to be their 'clothes horse'. At your signal to start, they take it in turns to throw the dice. They must throw certain numbers in order to clothe their volunteer: Boots = 1 (must be thrown once for each boot), Hat = 2, Sweatshirt = 3, Belt = 4, Coat = 5, Bible = 6.

The sweatshirt must be collected before the belt, and both must be worn before the coat goes on top. The Bible can only be collected when all the other garments are in place on the volunteer. The winning team is the one which is the first to completely dress and equip their volunteer.

Top tip!

To avoid any cheating, and to ensure that the clothes are collected and put on in the right order, have one leader with each team playing.

Theme points

Look at the clothes. A hat protects your head. Salvation protects what's inside your head! Now look at the other labels and work out why they are there – what do YOU think?

6 Balloon Drop

Themes

Emotions and feelings, peace

Bible link

John 14:27

You will need

Inflated balloons (put them all inside an old duvet cover for ease of storage/transport), indelible felt-tip pens for writing on the balloons (try one beforehand to make sure the ink doesn't run/rub off).

To play

Game 1 – Team quiz

Split into teams and get each team to choose a volunteer to be the team balloon holder. The volunteers stand together in a line in front of everyone. Ask the teams questions. If a team gets the answer right, they take a balloon from the sack, choose a negative emotion or feeling, and write it on the balloon. This is then given to the team balloon holder, who must not drop any balloons or the team is out. If the question is answered wrongly, or answered by another team, the team must take TWO balloons, label them and hand these to their balloon holder.

Play as quickly as possible – one leader could help with the balloon choosing and labelling while another keeps the questions and answers moving. Use simple Bible quiz questions, or silly trivia-type questions.

See who can achieve the record for holding the most balloons at once! Try holding them between teeth, under arms/chin etc. Repeat the game as often as you wish, reusing labelled balloons, then end with a mass balloon stomp, stamping on all the bad feelings until they've all gone.

Game 2 – Circle game

Sit round in a circle together and talk about bad feelings. Hand everyone a balloon to decorate with words or pictures that represent their own particular 'difficult' emotions – fear, anger, jealousy etc. Put the decorated balloons back in the bag, and play, in turns or pairs, a game of 'who can hold the most balloons at once', ending with a balloon stomp.

Children who do not like bursting balloons can stand back, ready to help you pick up the pieces to make your final point.

Top tip!

For the safety of your children, and anyone who may use the space a you, make sure you clear away all scraps of burst balloon.

Theme points

Pick up the tiny bits of balloon together – remember how they filled the duvet cover/bin liner a moment ago. Now they barely fill your hands. Jesus can get rid of our bad feelings just like this!

If you wish, hand everyone a new balloon to blow up and take home. Draw smiley faces and write 'PEACE' on them.

7 Beat the clock 7-9

Themes

Jesus' return, time for God

Bible

Matthew 14:22,23; Mark 1:35; 6:45,46; Luke 9:28

You will need

Either a wind-up kitchen timer, a small travel alarm clock or a wristwatch with an alarm setting.

To play

Explain that the alarm will be set to go off a short time after it has been hidden, but it could be set for any length of time from thirty seconds to three or four minutes – only the leader will know! The aim of the game is to find the timer before the alarm goes off.

If you're playing indoors, it can be hidden anywhere suitable – under books, behind chairs or curtains. The players will have to leave the room briefly while it is hidden.

If you are outdoors, the timer need not be too heavily concealed, or it might be too difficult to find in time!

Game 1 – Teams

Play in two teams, taking it in turns to hide the alarm. Score points for finding it before it goes off.

Game 2 – Individuals

Children take it in turns to find the timer, with the rest of the group remaining seated and chanting 'tick-tock, tick-tock!' Points could be scored for teams, with team members taking turns to 'Beat the clock'.

Game 3 – Whole group

Everyone searches for the timer together; whoever finds it can hide it for the next round.

Top tip!

Make sure you vary the time before the alarm goes off, making some rounds very short, as this adds to the urgency of the game.

Theme points

How did it feel looking for the timer? Knowing it could go off at any moment made it a bit of a jumpy experience. Jesus says he will come back again one day, but nobody knows when this will be.

You were racing against time to find the clock – our lives can be a race to do things 'in time', and it's easy to forget to make time for God.

8 Blow it!

Themes

Bible heroes, champions

You will need

Clean, two-litre plastic bottle (cap and labels removed), washing-up bowl containing a couple of inches of water, two buckets, one full of water, plastic jug for refilling bottle, one large bendy drinking straw per player.

To play

Play this on the floor, with the players on their knees round the washing-up bowl. Appoint a timekeeper. Fill the bottle with water, and (keeping your finger over the end) upend it in the bowl so that the mouth of the bottle is covered by the water in the bowl. The water should stay in the bottle! Their challenge is to see who can blow ALL the water out of the bottle in the shortest time possible!

Give each player a straw. One at a time, they should kneel at the bowl, and put the short end of their straw underwater and into the bottle neck – be sure to hold the bottle firmly in place (leaders might need to lend a hand here). The timekeeper then gives the command to 'Blow it!' and the player blows as hard as they can, until the bottle is empty. Note the player's name, and time taken, empty some of the water out of the bowl into a bucket, refill the bottle, and play on.

Top tip!

If playing indoors, spread newspaper or old towels across your playing area to guard against spills.

Theme points

This is a game of surprises. The first surprise to many children is that the water stays in the bottle, even upside down.

The second surprise is that it isn't always the obvious person who is good at this game – sustained efforts empty the bottle faster than huge showy short puffs!

God's champions are often 'unlikely people', who we can overlook, but their quiet, sustained efforts achieve results.

9 Boomerang bonanza

Themes

Trinity, Bible heroes

This is a visual reminder of the Trinity, used as a game that can be taken home for further fun and an ongoing reminder. Alternatively, use as a 'championship' game – find your own champion boomerang thrower, and use as an introduction to a Bible hero/champion such as David, Gideon or Samson.

You will need

Thin card boomerang for each player (enlarge template overleaf) as a 'Trinity' visual aid, write 'Father', 'Son' and 'Holy Spirit' on the three arms of the boomerang, a suitable playing area.

To play

Cut the boomerangs out and colour them together. Write the owner's name on the back before you play to avoid arguments later.

Line the children up, and let them throw their boomerangs, two or three at a time. See whose boomerang flies the furthest. The trick is to hold it lightly between the fingers and flick it horizontally. See if anyone can develop the wrist flick that will make it come curving back again!

If you have enough supervision to do so safely, children will also enjoy being allowed to run around and throw them freely.

Theme points

Ask the children how it feels when their boomerang flies well. Just being a strong-armed thrower isn't enough – you need a carefully made boomerang, plus the knack of flicking it just the right way.

The Bible heroes mentioned weren't famous simply for being strong or powerful – it was how they used their skills for God that made them heroes.

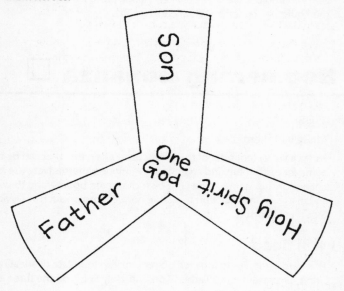

10 Bread

Themes

Bread of life, Lord's Supper, feeding of the five thousand, Harvest

Bible link

Matthew 14:13–21; 26:26–30; Mark 6:30–44; 14:22–26; Luke 9:10–17; 22:14–20; John 6:1–14,25–58; 1 Corinthians 10:16; 11:23–25

You will need

Clear playing space.

To play

For a team game, you will need a minimum of eight players. If your group is smaller than this, play with the whole group together for fun, without scoring points.

Divide your group into two teams, with an equal number of players in each team. The teams should line up, with the children standing in line behind each other. Tell them to put their hands on the shoulders of the child in front. This makes them into two 'loaves of bread' – each child is a slice in the loaf, and each 'loaf' is a complete team.

Explain that you are going to call out some actions, at random, which they must follow as quickly as possible. Practice these together. The actions are:

1 *Toast!* The slices break away individually, and jump up and down, as if popping out of the toaster.

2 *Rolls!* The slices crouch down with hands over heads.

3 *Sandwiches!* Pairs of slices (any team) stand face-to-face with hands up, pressed together.

4 *Pizza!* They lie flat on the floor.

5 *Loaves!* When this is called, all the slices must run and reassemble themselves back into their 'team' loaf. The first loaf completely reassembled wins a point.

Now play on, playing several times to see which team can earn the most points.

Theme points

In the game, you were pretending to be a few different kinds of bread. Can anyone think of some more? (Batons, pitta, naan, soda bread...) How many times a day do we/could we eat bread? What would we eat if there were no bread? What would life be like without bread?

When Jesus described himself as the 'bread of life', what was he telling us about himself? And about our need for him?

Also link with the Lord's Supper – 'This is my body, which is given for you.'

Substitute 'Fishes!' for 'Pizza!', to provide a link with the story of the feeding of the five thousand.

Use as a Harvest-related theme game.

11 Build up

Themes

Solomon's temple, building, living stones

Bible link

1 Kings 5–7; Ezra 3–6; 1 Peter 2:1–10

You will need

Tape or chalk, clear playing space, tokens for the teams to collect – these can be squares of paper, toys, balls etc.

To play

Chalk or tape two long parallel lines along the centre of your playing space, about one metre apart. This represents a wall. Place all the 'tokens' in a heap on the far side of the wall. Choose a volunteer to start the game as the catcher on the wall.

Divide the group into two teams, who start the game on the near side of the wall. Explain that everyone must run back and forth across the wall, fetching a token for their team each time they cross – these are placed in team piles at the starting point.

The catcher will tag anyone they can touch as the players run across the wall. Tagged players become 'bricks' in the wall, and have to stay where they are (leaders should take any tokens they may be holding when caught and return them to the main pile).

The remaining players have to dodge around the 'bricks' as the wall grows more 'solid'. If you wish, the bricks can stand with legs apart and arms stretched out to make the wall harder to cross.

Theme points

The wall in the game eventually became quite hard to cross – there were so many 'bricks' along the top. Everybody became part of the building of the wall. Who built the temple walls in Ezra? Everyone, all the Israelites, worked together.

Link with other 'building' stories, such as Solomon's temple – 1 Kings 5,6; Solomon's palace – 1 Kings 7; Nehemiah rebuilding the temple wall – Nehemiah 3,4.

Everyone became part of the wall in the game. We are told to become 'living stones' in God's hands (1 Peter 2:1–10), built into a 'temple' with Jesus as the foundation stone. What does this mean for us?

12 Burning bushes

Themes

Power of God, burning bush, pillar of fire, Holy Spirit, Pentecost

Bible link

Genesis 19:23–28; Exodus 3:2; 13:21,22; Numbers 11:1,2; 1 Kings 18:1–39; 2 Chronicles 7:1–3; Isaiah 43:2; Matthew 3:11; Luke 3:16; Acts 2:1–42; 7:30–34

You will need

Large playing space.

To play

Choose a volunteer to be the chaser. Explain that this is a simple game of tag, except that anyone who is tagged is set 'on fire', and becomes a burning bush. Bushes have to stay where they are, they cannot move, but their arms are flames waving around. Other players must take care not to run too close to any of the burning bushes, because if they are tagged by a flame, they too will be 'set on fire', and become a bush.

Play until everyone has been 'set on fire'. The last person to be tagged becomes the chaser for another round, if you wish.

Theme points

In the game you were only pretending to be 'on fire', so nobody was burned. The bush in Moses' story wasn't burned either – the fire represented the presence of God.

God sends fire on many occasions:

• As a sign of his presence and power. See Exodus 13:21,22; 40:34–38; 1 Kings 18:1–39; 2 Chronicles 7:1–3

• As a warning of displeasure at wrongdoing. See Numbers 11:2; Genesis 19:23–28;

• As a promise of power and purification. See Matthew 3:11; Luke 3:16; Acts 2.

Use the game to bring out any of these themes – instead of burning bushes, you can have the cities on the plain being struck by fire, pillars of fire, the Holy Spirit coming and touching everyone with tongues of fire etc.

13 Carpet chariot racing

Themes

Red sea crossing, Ahab and Jehoshaphat, Jehu and Ahaziah, Philip, Moses

Bible link

Exodus 14; 1 Kings 22:29–38; 2 Kings 9:14–28; Acts 8:26–40

You will need

Large playing space with smooth surface – polished wooden floors are ideal, offcuts of carpet cut into squares – rubber backed carpet is perfect as it gives the rider a good grip.

To play

Assemble 'chariot teams' of three players. Give each team a carpet square, and line them up on one side of your playing space. One team member should crouch down on the carpet square (carpet-side down), and hold their arms out to the other two team members. This is the 'chariot' and rider. The two other team members should stand slightly in front of the chariot, holding one of the charioteer's hands each. These are the 'horses'.

The charioteer must stay in a crouching position, leaning back slightly, and on the word 'go', the horses must pull their chariots and race across to the far side of the room, around a mark on the floor (or a chair, or a leader) and back to the start. Now swap places within the teams, so that everyone gets to have a ride in the 'chariot'.

Theme points

This could link in with retelling the stories of Philip and the Ethiopian; Pharaoh's army in chariots chasing Moses and the Israelites; King Jehu and Ahaziah; or Ahab and Jehoshaphat.

Top tip!

This is a very popular, if rowdy, game. It's helpful if all the teams are fairly evenly matched in terms of having a selection of people of different sizes and weight. Smaller children enjoy being towed around by bigger ones, as they can go quite fast. Keep an eye on things to see that nobody gets over-enthusiastic!

Variation:

To play

Each skater should remove their shoes, as it is easier to keep their feet on the 'skates'. Give each skater two squares of carpet ('skates') and use these carpet-side down.

Line them up, and see how fast they can skate across the room, around a chair and back, by sliding their carpet skates alternately forwards. Play for fun, or as a team relay race.

Theme points

Use this linked with a quiz game – children have to 'skate' across the room in relays to fetch a simple quiz question, piled on a table or chair, for their team. They skate back and hand them to a leader to read out to the team.

The team answers the question, and the next skater goes off, until all the questions have been answered. See which team finishes first. With a small group just play for fun as a 'skating quiz'.

Alternatively

Try playing this with a home-made jigsaw puzzle relay, by collecting bits of magazine pictures that have been cut up prior to the game. Team members must skate across to fetch the puzzle pieces, one at a time, for the team to reassemble. Try to match the number of puzzle pieces to the number of children in a team. Tie into the theme of recognising people and recognising Jesus.

14 Carried away!

Theme

Healing

Bible link

Matthew 4:24; 8:5–13; 9:1–8; Mark 2:1–12; Luke 5:17–26; 6:17–19; John 5:1–9; Acts 3:1–22; 8:4–8; 9:32–35

You will need

Clear playing space.

To play

Divide your group into threes or into two teams. Show them how two people can make a safe carrying seat for the third, by clasping wrists firmly (see illustration). The lightest member of the trio sits on the 'seat', and puts their arms around the necks of the other two. Practise making seats and carrying each other on them, for a few minutes.

When everyone is ready, line up your teams/trios, and have races across the playing space, carrying the 'lame' team member.

The leader should stand on the opposite side of the room, and when the trios reach the far side, the 'lame' member of the team must touch a leader. They can now all join hands and race back to the starting point.

Either play as a straightforward race game between sets of three children, with children taking it in turns to be carried, or have a team relay race, and see which team can be the fastest to carry all its members in turn to be 'healed'.

Top tip!

Most children should be able to carry another child for a short distance like this, but make sure you set the distance according to the particular age and abilities of the children in your group.

Theme points

How was your 'lame' team member 'healed'? By touching a leader. How were the lame and paralysed people in the stories healed? Some people were healed by being touched, others simply needed a word of healing – from Jesus, Peter or Philip. The power to heal comes from God, the Holy Spirit.

15 Chair or wall?

Theme

Choices, Joshua

Bible link

Joshua 24:14–24; Colossians 3:15

You will need

Clear playing space with a wall or other marker at one end, two chairs – one at the starting point and one halfway between the starting point and the wall, coin.

To play

Game 1 – Whole group

Explain that this game is a running race with a difference. It is played two at a time, so ask for a pair of volunteers to start the game.

Explain that you will toss a coin to see who will choose 'chair or wall'. Choosing 'chair' means that on the word 'go', that player must run and touch the chair in the centre, run back to base and touch that chair, then run and touch the wall and back to base again. Choosing 'wall' means that the player must run first to the wall, then base, then the centre chair, then back to base. Once one player has chosen their run, the other must make the opposite run, with both players running at the same time. Whichever player finishes their run first is the winner of that run.

Game 2 – Teams

For a team game, divide the group into two teams, with each team sending a player to make a run against the other, teams taking it in turns to choose 'chair' or 'wall'. Play for points, if you wish.

Top tip!

Try to match the runners equally. In the team version, let the teams take it in turns to put a player forward for the other team to choose a challenger – players can only run once, so they need to choose carefully!

Theme points

The choices in this game were quite simple, and in fact, didn't affect the outcome much as both runners had to cover exactly the same distance. The choice of team runners may have made some difference.

What choices do we have to make in life, eg friends, clothes, TV, how we behave, how hard we work? What difference do these choices make to us? How do we make choices like these? See Colossians 3:15 for some useful advice.

Joshua told the Israelites that God would be good to them if they chose to serve him. It was up to them to choose how they would live, and they would have to live with the consequences if they made the wrong choice (Joshua 24).

16 Chair play!

Themes

God made us, creation

Bible link

Genesis 2; Psalm 139

You will need

One set of the following items per group of three to five children: stacking chair (or similar), hat, zip-front jacket, trousers (ideally elastic-waisted), pair of shoes or boots, inflated balloon.

To play

This is played in a relay race to build a complete figure. At one end of the room are each team's clothes. The players line up in their teams at the opposite end, with a chair, and take it in turns to run and fetch an item of clothing. When they return with it, each member of the team must put it on and then take it off, passing it down the line, until it reaches the end.

Then they start to 'dress' their chair, with the front legs inside the trouser legs, the coat zipped up over the chair back, a shoe on each of the front feet and a hat on a balloon head. Take care to zip the jacket completely, in order to wedge the balloon safely in the neck. See which team can be the first to create a complete 'Chairperson'!

Faces can be drawn on the balloons at the end, and the chairs lined up to vote for 'most realistic chairperson', 'scruffiest chairperson' etc.

Theme points

The players had fun creating some marvellous 'chairpeople', putting all the parts together and creating a new figure every time. No two figures were exactly the same. God made us much more carefully! He put us together to make special, individual people of each one of us all.

17 Christmas grand slam

Theme

Christmas

You will need

One identical set of pictures per team (cut from magazines, old Christmas cards or pictures drawn by yourself or the children) enough in the set so there is one picture per clue plus a few extra, list of seasonal clues:

1. Something you sing at Christmas (*Carols*)
2. They followed a star at Christmas (*Magi/wise men*)
3. Something you eat at Christmas (*Turkey/mince pies*)
4. Something you hang up at Christmas (*Decorations*)
5. It shone in the sky at Christmas (*Star*)
6. We give these at Christmas (*Presents*)
7. Something shiny at Christmas (*Decorations/star*)
8. They were in the fields at Christmas (*Sheep/shepherds*)
9. A baby's bed at Christmas (*Manger*)
10. He has a red nose at Christmas (*Rudolph/Santa*)
11. Mary rode on this (*Donkey*)
12. Ring these at Christmas (*Bells*)

Make up as many 'fun' clues as possible.

To play

Place two jumbled up sets of pictures on two separate tables, or spread them on the floor some distance apart from each other.

Divide the group into two teams; invite a volunteer from each team to come forward. Explain that you are going to read out some Christmassy clues. As soon as you have read the clue out, the first two volunteers must run to their team picture pile and find the appropriate picture.

Some clues might have more than one possible picture answer, this doesn't matter – they must grab a possible picture, run back to you and slam it on the table. Whoever gets there first, with an appropriate picture, wins a point for their team.

Now compare pictures – if both teams have chosen the same picture, they both get another point.

Replace the pictures in the team piles and play again with another pair of volunteers.

Top tip!

Make the game more of a challenge by providing lots of extra pictures per team, so the children have a greater choice.

Theme points

Some of the pictures were directly related to the Bible story of Christmas, while others were not. Yet we associate all of the pictures with Christmas! Discuss this, beginning by asking the children to help you sort the pictures out.

Go through them all together, and ask the group to tell you which pile they belong in – Bible story pictures or 'Christmassy things'. Why do we have Christmassy things like these? Point out that Christmas is a celebration of God's gift to us, Jesus.

The other things in the pile are like party things – they have been added on over the years as people have celebrated Christmas together in many different ways. There's nothing wrong with that, unless we lose sight of the real meaning of Christmas under the pile of party things.

Illustrate this by putting the 'Bible' pile first under, then on top of the other pile.

18 Circle games

Themes

God made us, abilities, disabilities

Bible link

Genesis 2; Psalm 139

You will need

Two or more balls, one tennis ball-sized, one football-sized (foam sponge balls are ideal, and make the games easier to play).

To play

Everyone should be seated on chairs, in a close circle. There are three games to play, in fairly quick succession, in order to make the theme points at the end. All three games involve passing the balls around the circle.

For a simple game, use one ball; for a more exciting game with older or more able children you could use two or more balls at once, depending on the size of the circle.

Nobody must leave their seats at any point; a leader should retrieve any balls that roll away, and the game then starts again from the beginning.

Game 1 – No hands!

Pass the football(s) around the circle, each player passing the ball to the person seated on their immediate left. Only feet may be used to hold or dribble the ball, and there is no wild kicking allowed – show the red card to any of these players! See how quickly you can pass the ball all the way around. If space permits, you could try moving the chairs back into a slightly bigger circle and playing again.

Game 2 – No feet!

Play exactly as before, only this time no feet are allowed to touch the ball – hands only.

Game 3 – No hands, no feet!

Use tennis balls, and keep the chairs very close together. The balls must be passed around the circle using no hands or feet – pass them by holding between chins and chests. Try again, using footballs and knees.

Theme points

Which version was the easiest? Probably the hands-only version, as we use our hands for so many things. Which version was the hardest? Probably the last one, when neither hands or feet could be used.

God gave us bodies with all the parts we need for living. He knows how much we need all the things that make us 'who we are'.

CAUTION!

Disabled children may struggle with this concept – if God makes everyone perfectly, why are people deaf, blind, lame, ill etc. You may need to discuss the fact that we live in an imperfect world, and that we are ALL affected by that in some way, and that physical disabilities are part of living in a 'fallen' world. Nevertheless, God has plans for us all and can use us just as we are. Our disabilities are part of our own uniqueness.

19 Coin drop

Themes

Giving, widow's offering, money

Bible link

Matthew 6:24; Mark 12:41–44; Luke 16:13; 21:1–4

You need

Plastic bucket, almost full of water, pound coin (or 20p), supply of
2p coins

To play

This game is extremely popular and addictive, as the players cannot
believe how hard it is and want to keep coming back to try again!

Have the children sit or stand round in a circle. Put the bucket of water
in the centre. Show the children the pound coin, and place it in the
bottom of the bucket, in the middle. Now explain that anyone who can
drop a 2p coin into the water so that it completely covers the pound
coin can keep it!

Allow children, in turns, to come forward and drop a 2p coin – have as
many turns as you wish, retrieving dropped coins for reuse from time to
time.

If your group is large, you may wish to divide it into teams, with one
leader and bucket per team, so that everyone gets an opportunity to
have a go.

Theme points

The game looked easier than it was. Why did everyone want to keep on
trying? First of all, to prove it could be done, but also because they
wanted to win the money. Why is money attractive?

The widow had very little, but was willing to give all of it away. How did
this make her different from most (richer) people?

20 Corners ▢

Theme

Safety

Bible link

Joel 2:32; Acts 2:21; Romans 10:13

You will need

Large, clear playing space – mark the corners with cones or chairs if necessary.

To play

Divide into four groups, and ask for a volunteer to be the chaser. The chaser could wear a hat, to distinguish them from the runners. The four groups are sent to the four corners of the playing area; as long as they are in a corner they are safe.

The chaser stands in the middle, and the leader blows a whistle (or shouts 'go'). Everyone must run to the diagonally opposite corner without being tagged. Anyone who is tagged is out until the next game. When all the remaining players are in their new corners, play is repeated, until there is only one person left, who becomes the new chaser in the middle.

As long as play moves fast and new games begin again quickly, nobody should be out of the game for very long. In a very small playing space, this works better if the chaser is blindfolded first!

Theme points

It was 'safe' in the corners – was it hard leaving them? You had to run fast to the next safe place to try to stay in the game. Sometimes life is a bit like this. We go from places where we feel safe, through places where we feel not so safe (where are these?) until we reach another place where we feel really safe again.

How does Jesus make us feel safe? How can we find safety with him?

21 Cornerstones

Theme

Books of the Bible

You will need

Bibles; large pieces of paper taped up in each corner of the room, with the words NEW, OLD, BEFORE, AFTER on; pre-prepared list of books of the Bible or Bible index for you.

To play

Play either as teams or pairs, competing in turns, or as a group activity. Give out the Bibles, or the photocopied index pages. Explain that you are going to play a game that will test how well they know their way around the Bible. They will have a few minutes to look at the list of books in the Bible, and then you will test them on how much they can remember!

Hand out Bibles, and give them a few minutes to look at the index. Collect them in again and have everyone stand together in the middle of the room. Explain that the corner labelled OLD represents the Old Testament; the opposite corner (labelled NEW) represents the New Testament.

You are going to say the name of a book in the Bible. They must dash to either the 'Old' or 'New' corner, depending on where they think it belongs. Now name another book of the Bible. Does this come before or after the one you've just mentioned? They should dash again to the correct corner.

The game can now continue with the same sequence – old or new? Before or after? If they struggle, let them keep the index and make it a race to see who can find the right answer and run to the correct corner first.

Top tip!

You could play this as a rolling knockout game, with pairs of children competing – when one runs to the wrong corner, they are replaced by another volunteer. See who can stay in the longest, and give everyone a fair chance by choosing easy or difficult to remember books as appropriate.

Theme points

The Bible is a collection of 'books' written at different times. What is the difference between the Old and New Testaments?

22 Crazy castles

Themes

Tower of Babel, Solomon's temple, Nehemiah, building, Jericho

Bible link

Genesis 11:1–9; Joshua 6; 1 Kings 6; Nehemiah 3; Matthew 7:24–27;
Luke 6:46–49; 14:28

You will need

For the tabletop game: Selection of small flat objects, eg CD cases,
tablemats, playing cards, books, matchboxes, videos, notebooks, plastic
boxes, paper plates, envelopes... anything that is suitable for piling up
and falling down.

For the floor game: Selection of fairly large objects, eg cardboard boxes,
books, plastic crates, laundry baskets, large soft toys, cushions etc.

For the edible version: Selection of plain biscuits of assorted shapes and
sizes (be aware of food allergies). Wash hands first for this one, and build
on a tray!

To play

Game 1 – Tabletop game

All the players sit round a table within reach of the collection of small
objects. They take it in turns to take an object and place it in the centre
of the table, each successive object on top of the previous one. See how
high you can build before the pile falls down, then start again, with a
different person starting the building.

Game 2 – Floor game

Players take it in turns to build a tower with the larger objects, as in
Game 1, starting again when the tower collapses.

Game 3 – Edible version

All the players sit round a tray on the table, and build with biscuits,
seeing how high they can get before the pile falls over. When everyone
has had a go at starting the pile, hand round drinks and have a break,
eating the debris!

Theme points

Discuss how building looks easy before you start, but gets harder as you go on. It takes patience, care and persistence – relate this to your Bible story.

Your towers all fell down eventually – no building made by man lasts for ever. Relate the game to Joshua/Jericho. Your building fell down because it wasn't very well made. Why did the walls of Jericho fall down?

Foundations matter, too. Getting the base objects right affects the height and stability of your building – relate this to the wise man who builds on rock (Matthew 7:24–27).

Talk about Nehemiah, and the team effort involved in building.

Play all three versions of the game at different points of your group session for greatest impact.

23 Creeping lions

Themes

Daniel in the lions' den, God's protection, trusting God

Bible link

Daniel 6

You will need

Large, clear playing space.

To play

Choose a volunteer to be Daniel, and explain that the rest of the group are to be lions. Daniel spent a night in a den with lions and he was unharmed, so all the lions are going to go to sleep! All the lions are to go and lie down somewhere in your playing space. They must stay flat on the floor the whole time. Daniel stands in the middle of this circle of sleeping lions – he can turn around, but must stay in the centre at all times. The lions must remain absolutely motionless while Daniel is looking at them, but at the same time, they must try to inch forwards while he is not looking. Daniel must watch all the lions as closely as he can – if he spots one moving, that lion is out, until the next round of the game. If a lion manages to wriggle close enough to Daniel to touch his foot, Daniel is out, and they change places. Play starts again from the beginning.

Alternatively, play a team version, with the lions belonging to different teams. The teams lose a point if any of its members are spotted moving, and they gain ten points for touching Daniel.

Top tip!

Strong refereeing is needed here! Be strict but fair in your decisions, keeping the game moving fast, and promising another round of play for everyone if they cooperate!

Theme points

The lions remained 'asleep' because they wanted to win the game – why did the lions in the story leave Daniel unharmed? What does this tell us about God? What does this tell us about Daniel?

24 Crossing the Jordan 7-9

Themes

Joshua, Moses, Crossing the Jordan, Crossing the Red Sea.

Bible link

Exodus 14; Joshua 3,4

You will need

Clear playing space; chalk or masking tape.

To play

Draw or tape lines across the floor dividing your playing space into three equal sections. The centre space is the river (or sea).

All the players line up along one edge of the river. Choose a volunteer to be Joshua (or Moses), who stands in the river. All the players chant aloud, 'Joshua, Joshua, may we cross the Jordan?' (or 'Moses, Moses, may we cross the Red Sea?') Joshua replies, 'Not yet!'

The players then repeat their request, and Joshua replies, 'Only if you're wearing... (*names any colour*).' Any player who has something on them with that colour on it may now walk safely across the river to the opposite bank. Any player without something that colour, must try to rush across without being tagged, or walk, and try to bluff their way across. If a player is caught, and doesn't have the colour, they join Joshua in the river trying to tag players in the next crossing.

Repeat the chanting/crossing back across the river. Play on until the last person left untagged becomes the next 'Joshua' – the leader's decision is final!

Theme points

It was only safe to cross the river (or sea) in your game if you could show that you had the right colour. What made it safe to cross the river or sea in the stories of Joshua and Moses? Who made this happen? How did the Israelites feel about what happened? What effect did it have on their enemies?

25 Crossover

Themes

Sin, Jesus the way, salvation

Bible link

John 11:25,26; 14:6; 1 John 4:10

You will need

Clear playing space, chalk or tape, hat or baseball cap for each team.

To play

Mark out two parallel lines across the middle of your playing space, about a metre apart. The space between these lines is the 'wall'. Choose a volunteer to be a catcher on the wall. Divide the rest of your group into teams of four or more. The more teams there are, the better. The aim is to be the first team to get all of its members safely across the wall.

Each team chooses a captain to start the game, and the captains all wear hats. Team members may only cross the wall one at a time, holding hands with their team captain. The catcher in the middle must try to tag the captains before they reach the far side. They can only be tagged while escorting another team member on the wall, and only captains can be tagged. Untagged captains leave their team member in safety, and run back across the wall to fetch another player. Tagged captains must give their hat to the player that they are escorting, and both return to the beginning and try again, with a new team captain.

Theme points

The wall in the game was just an imaginary one. However, there is a real wall between ourselves and God – it's called 'sin'. God is so holy we cannot approach him by ourselves (1 John 4:10). Jesus helps us to cross the wall. We are only able to approach God if we 'hold on' to Jesus (John 14:6). How can we do this?

The wall in the game was crossed with the help of the team captains, and only the captains could be tagged. Jesus was punished for our sins. He took our place, in order that we may be able to cross the wall from death to life with him (John 11:25,26). There is no other way across the wall.

26 Donkey riding

Theme

Palm Sunday

Bible link

Zechariah 9:9; Matthew 21:1–11; John 12:12–16

You will need

Large, clear playing space.

To play

Game 1 – Whole group

Pair the children up, putting a bigger child with a smaller one in each pair. Explain that the bigger child is going to be the donkey, and the other will be the rider. All the donkeys should get down on their hands and knees, while the riders get on their backs and hold on tightly, as they race across the playing space (make sure your playing space has a soft floor covering, like carpet or even grass!).

Play again, swapping the children around so that everyone can have a turn at riding, if possible. In a small group, race the donkeys two at a time for fun, with children choosing whether to be a donkey or a rider.

Game 2 – Teams

Divide the group into teams, who choose donkeys and riders to have a series of races against each other.

Top tip!

Watch the riders closely, and make sure that the donkeys don't go too fast for the riders to hold on safely. You may prefer to divide into threes, with one child as 'donkey handler', to lead the donkeys and ensure the rider's safety.

Theme points

Jesus entered Jerusalem on a donkey. Why did he choose to ride a donkey? It was a traditional sign of a king coming in peace – donkeys are not warlike creatures!

27 Don't say that!

Themes

Bible stories, Easter, Christmas

You will need

Whistle, bell or tin tray to bang.

To play

Explain that you are all going to take it in turns to tell each other the Christmas story (or the Easter story, or any other Bible story you have been studying recently). The catch is that some words are not allowed! Ask for your first volunteer. Ask them to start telling the story, but they must not use the word AND. See how far they can get, and when a mistake is made, blow the whistle or ring a bell, and get everyone to cheer. Alternatively, get everyone to shout, 'Boom-boom!' when a mistake is made – this keeps everyone listening to the storyteller. Congratulate your storyteller on the story so far, and ask for another volunteer.

Start again, this time without the word THE. Play on, changing the forbidden word each time – you could try HE, SHE, SO, BUT as well as AND and THE.

If they get too clever, try banning two or three words, in order to find a champion storyteller.

Top tip!

If the story never really gets going, try having each volunteer pick up where the previous one left off. You could also try playing this as a circle game. Pass the story around the circle to the next player each time a mistake is made, until the whole story has been told. To play this version, try giving the storyteller an object, eg a teddy bear, to hold whilst telling the story. The teddy must be passed on as soon as a mistake is made and the story passes on. Keep the game moving quickly and nobody will mind making a mistake – it's all part of the fun.

Theme points

Use as an introduction to your chosen theme/story. Did they get the facts right, as well as remembering not to use the buzzword?

28 Escape

Themes

Jonah, Goliath, David, escape, Herod, Saul, emotions, Christmas, Harvest.

Bible link

Jonah 1:3; 1 Samuel 17; Matthew 2:12,16; Acts 9:1

You will need

Large, clear playing space.

To play

Ask for a volunteer to be the first chaser. Explain that everyone must hold on to the chaser, and only run away when he says the buzzword. The chaser holds his arms out and everyone holds on to an arm or a finger. The chaser calls out the names of the other players at random, but at any moment he chooses, adds 'Jonah!', which is the signal for everyone to run away. Whoever is tagged becomes the next chaser. Anyone who lets go too soon is out for that round of the game.

Theme points

Jonah ran away from God. Why? What happened? Use as a discussion starter for the story of Jonah.

Use in the same way as a discussion starter for other Bible stories of people who either ran away, or caused others to run away, by changing the name you use as the buzzword, eg Herod, Goliath, Saul, David. Alternatively, use it to bring out any other theme point.

Anger: Start the game by using the phrase 'I got up today and I felt quite… happy, sad, tired, bored' running away on Angry! Talk about whether it is easy to run away from anger? How do we deal with it?

For a seasonal link, use related buzzwords, such as Crackers! ('At Christmas time I think of…') or Bread ('At Harvest time we thank God for…').

29 Fishes in the net

Themes

Following Jesus, fishers of men, captivity, freedom

Bible link

Isaiah 61:1; Matthew 4:18–20; Mark 1:16–20; Luke 4:18; 5:1–11;
John 8:31–36

You will need

Large, clearly defined playing space, whistle for leader.

To play

Ask for two volunteers to hold hands, with arms outstretched. Explain
that these two are fishermen, holding a net. The rest of the children are
'fishes', and must run around within your playing space, and try to avoid
being caught in the net. On the word 'go', the fishermen run about,
holding hands, their arms stretched out between them, and try to trap
the fishes by encircling them up in their 'net'. The leader needs to watch
the game closely, and blow a whistle or otherwise indicate when a fish is
deemed to have been netted.

Caught fishes are out of the game – you could designate one end of
your space a 'pond' where they are kept until they are released back into
the river for the next round.

Set a time limit, and see how many fishes your fishermen can catch in
that time, and then start again, with a new pair of fishermen.

Theme points

Simon Peter, James, John, and Andrew were fishermen when Jesus
called them. They dropped their nets and left everything they had
to follow him. You were actually catching people, not fishes! Jesus
promised he would make his followers 'fishers of men'. What did
he mean?

The net trapped the fishes, who got in a bit of a tangle in the process.
What kind of things can trap us, and get us in a tangle in our lives? Bad
habits, the wrong kind of friends, spending too much money etc. There
are many things that can trap us like fishes in a net. Jesus promises to
set us free, if we turn to him for help.

30 Follow your leader

Theme

Following Jesus

Bible link

Matthew 4:19; 8:22; 9:9; 16:24; Mark 2:14; 8:34; 10:21; Luke 5:27; 9:23; John 12:26

You will need

Lively music, simple obstacle course (use tables, chairs, cushions etc).

To play

Game 1 – Whole group

All the children line up – the child at the front of the line is the leader. The leader moves forward and around the room – under, over and around the obstacles – while the rest of the children must all follow exactly where the leader goes. The leaders should also perform a series of actions as they go along, eg wave their left arm then their right, jump to the left then the right, turn right round, pat themselves on the head. The rest of the line must copy the movements exactly, in a ripple effect down the line, with each child copying the one immediately in front.

Let the children take turns to be the leader, changing over when the music stops, with the leader going to the back of the line, until everyone has had a turn.

Game 2 – Teams

Divide the group into small teams of four or five children. Play as before, with all the teams moving around the obstacle course together, following their team leader's actions. Change team leaders as above.

47

Theme points

Talk together about how some leaders were easier to follow than others – some moved too quickly, performed complicated actions etc. To play the game, you had no choice but to follow the leader.

Jesus gives us a choice – we don't have to follow him. If we do, though, he will help us safely through and around all the things we come across in our lives. How can we also copy his actions as we go?

31 Full pelt

This is a good opening game for children who arrive full of energy and need to let off some steam safely before you begin.

Themes

John the Baptist, starter game, emotions and feelings

Bible link

Isaiah 40:3; Matthew 3:3; Hebrews 12:1

You will need

Small foam tennis balls – the more, the better (make your own small sock balls from clean, old socks/tights, rolled in on themselves and secured with a couple of stitches), lots of empty plastic soft drink bottles of all shapes and sizes, thick black marker pen suitable for writing on plastic, table or line of tables at one end of a large, clear playing space.

To play

As the children arrive, hand them an empty bottle each, and ask them to think of something that they know is a bad way to feel or act (for example, telling lies, fighting). Ask them to write their words on the bottle (leaders may need to help children decide what to write).

The bottles should then be lined up on a table at the far side of the playing space, and each child should be given a ball. Count to three, and then all the balls should be thrown at the table with the aim of knocking all the bottles over. Once the balls have been thrown, children can run to the table, stand the bottles up, run back to the throwing line and play again.

Give bottles and balls to late arrivals as they come in, and let them join in at the next opportunity.

Theme points

It is very satisfying throwing balls as hard as you can, and clearing the rubbish off the table. Jesus wants us to let him clear the rubbish out of our lives. How can we let him do this? Just as the bottles could be picked up and put back on the table, we can all get angry, tell lies, and do other bad things again and again – sometimes it happens without us meaning to do it. We need to keep on asking Jesus to clear away our rubbish.

Link this also with John the Baptist, who came to clear a way for Jesus.

32 Getaway!

Themes

Captives, release, helping others, rescue, escape

Bible link

Acts 5:17–25; 12:1–11; 16:16–40

You will need

Large playing space with a wall at one side.

To play

Choose a player to be the 'jailer'. Explain to the group that this is a simple tag game, but any player who is tagged by the jailer must go and stand with an arm outstretched, touching the wall. These players are now 'chained' to the prison wall in a line. They can only be set free by an untagged player coming and running under all the arms, at the risk of being caught and tagged themselves! Play until all the players are chained to the wall, and then get the jailer to run under the tunnel of arms to set everyone free. The last player to be caught becomes the new jailer for another game, if you wish.

Top tip!

Keep a close eye on the action, to make sure that all tagged players go to prison, and only leave when properly released. In a large group, it may help to have two or three jailers – start with one, and if it is impossible to keep any prisoners appoint extra ones.

Theme points

How did your prisoners escape from their chains? Who released Paul/Peter/the apostles? Who sent the angels/earthquakes? The other Christians were praying for those held captive – God answered their prayers. In the game, everyone had a part to play in helping the others stay free. How can we help other Christians who are in trouble?

33 Gotcha!

Themes

People in the Bible, places in the Bible, Christmas, Easter, Harvest, names

You will need

Rolled-up newspaper.

To play

All the players should sit on chairs, in a fairly large circle. One player stands in the middle with a rolled-up newspaper. Explain that one of the seated players will start the game by calling out the name of another seated player. The batter must try to hit the knees/legs of the named player before they in turn name another player. Players have to keep their ears open and listen for their names to be called, and be ready to call someone else's name quickly to avoid being caught. Keep it moving fast. Any player who is caught out before naming someone else changes place with the batter.

Keep an eye on this game and don't let any children get too 'overenthusiastic' when they are the batter!

Theme points

Change the theme to suit your needs:

• Bible people – every child takes the name of someone in the Bible. It may help to keep a list of these visible in case they can't think of a name to call. Discuss afterwards who they all were, finally focusing on your particular personality from your current Bible story.

• Bible places – as above, but using Biblical place names.

• Christmas – every child takes the name of something associated with Christmas, such as holly, robins, tree, star etc. Afterwards, talk about why we associate these things with Christmas. Which are important and why?

• Easter – as above, using words associated with Easter.

• Harvest – children can choose fruit and vegetable names. Then play again, with the children choosing any object they like. Point out that everything we have comes from God's provision, including all the raw materials from which everything we need is made.

• Names – once they have got to know each other's names, play a fun version with them all taking the name of the child seated to their left. Real concentration is needed for this one!

34 Grapevine

Themes

Jesus the Vine, fruit of the Spirit

Bible link

John 15:1–17; Galatians 5:22,23

You will need

Inflated balloons with one of the following words written on: Love, Joy, Peace, Patience, Kindness, Goodness, Faithfulness, Humility, Self-Control (store in an old duvet cover or bin liner), indelible felt-tip pen (OHP pens are ideal), string or wool cut into one-metre lengths, a chair.

To play

Game 1 – Whole group

Explain that the balloons represent the fruit of the Spirit. Does anyone know what these are? Show them the words. Give each child a length of string, asking for a volunteer to come forwards. Ask if they can transport all the 'fruit' to the other side of your playing space, using only the string, and without tying any balloons up? It's impossible!

Now show them how, if they all stand in a circle, with the child opposite holding the other end of their piece of string, the whole group together can make a 'net' which will hold all the balloons! Drop one balloon into the net – which symbolises the 'grapevine'– and challenge them to cross the room, round a chair, and get back without dropping the balloon. They will need to cooperate to keep the strings pulled tightly to support the balloon. Each time they go round, add another balloon. See how much fruit your vine can bear before it starts to fall apart!

Game 2 – Teams

In larger groups, play in two teams, racing to see which team can grow the most fruit without losing any on the way.

Theme points

Why couldn't one player carry all those balloons alone? 'A branch cannot produce fruit unless it stays joined to the vine' (John 15:4). All the players needed to remain united in order to carry the balloons. We need to remain united with Jesus in order to carry the fruit of the Spirit in our lives, then we will 'produce lots of fruit' (John 15:5).

35 Haul away!

Themes

Giving, Sharing

Bible link

Acts 2:43–47; 4:32; 11:27–30; 1 Corinthians 16:1–4; 2 Corinthians 8:1–15; 9:1–15

You will need

Large cardboard box for each team (supermarket fruit boxes are ideal) with a very long length of string attached to two (opposite) sides, various objects for transporting in the boxes – soft toys, food cans, clothing, books (as many objects as there are members in each team) – pile these up behind the teams, or leave space to have to run to fetch objects.

To play

Divide your group into two or more teams and line the teams up on one side of the playing space. Explain that you are going to imagine that one member of each team has gone to live overseas, and needs support from home. One member of each team goes to sit on the ground at the far side of your playing space. This can be as large as you like. Place a box each in front of the teams.

The first player in each team should take hold of their end of the string. Pull out the string on the opposite side of the box, and take it to their respective 'overseas' volunteers. Explain that these are the 'parcels' that will be sent overseas. At the moment they are empty, and it's up to the teams to race to supply their volunteers with all they need. On the word 'go', team members take it in turns to fetch an object from the heap, and place it in the box. They wave to their overseas member, who must haul the box across the room, and remove the object before the box is hauled back. The next team member selects an object etc, until everyone has sent something overseas. See which team can be the first to finish.

If everyone wants to have another go, you could play again in reverse, changing sides, until everything has been sent back again.

Theme points

Discuss why and how we could support Christians in other countries, or those in need.

36 Help! ⬚

Themes

Help, captivity, bullying, rescue, cooperation

Bible link

2 Chronicles 20:1–30; Psalm 46; Acts 2:21; Hebrews 13:6

You will need

Simple version

Two 'flags' – use coloured scarves or sheets of A4 paper.

Extended version

Two flags (as simple version), an assortment of 'trophies' of equal number for each team such as coloured balls, hats, soft toys – anything that can be easily grabbed, a taped or chalked line down the middle of the playing space.

To play

Divide your group into two teams, and send them to stand either side of your dividing line. These are their 'team bases' and they cannot be tagged whilst in their own base. Each team has a flag, which must be placed on the ground, towards the back of the team playing space. The aim of the game is to capture the flag of the opposite team, and return it to team base without being tagged by a member of the opposing team.

Anyone who is tagged whilst attempting to capture the flag is made a prisoner, and must stand behind the flag and call 'Help!' Prisoners are released by being tagged by one of their own team members and all captured team members must be released before the flag can be taken. See how long it takes for a flag to be captured, or for every member of one team to be taken captive.

For a longer game, line up some 'trophies' along with the flag, which have to be captured too – once captured, they are placed with the team's own trophies, where they may be recaptured at any time. The game finishes when one team has all of the trophies, or all of its members are captive. This is a very exciting and fast-moving game that ideally needs several referees to step in quickly to sort out disagreements and keep the playing light-hearted. Teams that work together do better.

Theme points

How did the captives feel when they were caught? It was good to be able to call for help from other team members. What happened when Judah was invaded? (2 Chronicles 20) How can we let God fight our battles for us? When do we need his help in our lives?

37 Jesus 'rules' OK!

Themes

Commandments, loving one another

Bible link

Exodus 20:1–17; Deuteronomy 5:1–22; John 13:34

Game 1 – Fan the kipper

You will need

One folded newspaper and one cut-out paper 'kipper' per team.

To play

Divide the group into teams, with a minimum of three per team. Line everyone up on one side of the room with their newspapers and kippers. On the word 'go', they take it in turns to fan their kippers across the room, until they touch the far side wall. They then fan them back again, and the next team member takes a turn. All team members sit down when they finish. Kippers are not allowed to be touched by hands, feet, or folded newspapers. All kippers must touch the far side wall before returning.

You will need

One table tennis ball and a tablespoon for each team.

To play

Balancing the table tennis ball on the tablespoon, the aim is to touch the wall and return without dropping the ball, and then hand the spoon and ball to the next team member. Holding the ball with fingers or thumbs is not allowed. If a ball is dropped, that player must go back to the start and begin again. Whatever game you choose to play, play once or twice, and then announce that there aren't any rules any more. Play again, reminding them that they can play however they like. Call a halt before things become too fraught.

Theme points

Ask what happened when they could play how they liked? What differences do rules make? Which version did they prefer? Why? Rules makes games enjoyable for everyone, not just a few. The whole point of the game is lost without rules. This is why God has given us 'Rules for living'. He wants us all to enjoy life, and rules are necessary to make life enjoyable and safe for everyone. What are these rules called? (The Ten Commandments.) Jesus tells us that there is one rule to remember above all others – love one another. If we keep this rule, we will keep all the others too!

38 Living words

Themes

Memory verses, God's Word

Bible link

Jeremiah 36, Hebrews 4:12

You will need

Large blackboard and chalks or large whiteboard and whiteboard marker, a damp sponge or similar; suitable Bible text, eg, 'What God has said isn't only alive and active! It is sharper than any double-edged sword.' (Hebrews 4:12)

To play

For a race, you will need a board and sponge for each team, otherwise play as a whole-group activity.

Begin by propping the board securely in front of the group. Line the group up, seated in single file, facing the board. Explain that you are going to write up a memory verse for them to read out loud. When you have written the verse out, hand the sponge to the child at the front of the seated line of players. Ask them to read the verse out, as loudly as possible. As soon as they finish reading it out, the player with the sponge must jump up, rub out any one word of the verse, hand the sponge to the next player in line, and then run to sit at the back of the line. Everyone must shout the complete verse again, including the missing word, before the next player jumps up and rubs a word out, and so on, until the board is bare again. Now ask the group to recite the entire verse from beginning to end, and write it up again as they do so – can they remember the chapter and verse as well?

For a team game, play as a race between teams, each team having a different verse. You will need a leader to oversee each team playing.

Theme points

The king burned the scroll that Jeremiah sent him (Jeremiah 36), but Jeremiah knew God's words so well that he was able to write them out again, from memory. In this game, the group was able to learn a few of God's words well enough to do this themselves. Why is it a good thing to be able to remember verses like this by heart? When could it be useful or helpful to us to know our Bibles this well? How can we begin to do this?

39 Map it out

Themes

Travelling, guidance, Jesus the way, people in the Bible

Bible link

Genesis 12,13; Exodus 13–19; Isaiah 30:21; John 14:6; Acts 13–28

You will need

Large scale maps – any map will do (world maps are fun, as long as the place names are fairly easy to read), slips of paper with place names on them (or the names of countries/local landmarks, depending on the kind of map you use), Blu-tack or pins.

To play

Pin the map up, or have it flat on a suitable surface.

Game 1 – Pairs

Let the children come forward in pairs, take a slip of paper with a place name and then locate that place on the map. They should stick their place name in the correct place. See how quickly they can do this – the rest of the group could count aloud to time them. Encourage them to help each other if they see someone struggling.

Game 2 – Team races

Divide the group into two teams. The children race in relays to take place names, fix them on the map and sit down again. Use two maps, one for each team.

Theme points

Talk about the difficulty of finding places you don't know, and how it helps to have someone to help and guide you. Who guided Moses, Abraham and Paul? Who can guide us through life? What 'map' can we use? (Bible) How can we find the way to God? See John 14:6 for a clue!

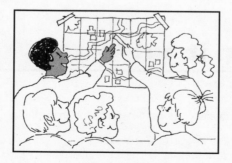

40 Martha and Mary

Themes

Peace, strength, Martha and Mary, listening to Jesus

Bible link

Isaiah 26:3; 40:31; Psalm 46:10,11; Luke 10:38–42

You will need

Memory verse of your choice, eg Luke 10:41,42 written out on a sheet of paper (optional).

To play

Have the group sit round in a circle. One person steps forward and says 'On the day that Jesus came to visit, Martha…' and adds something that Martha did, miming it at the same time. The second person repeats this line and adds another phrase and mime. Go around the circle, creating a longer and longer list of things that Martha did, which has to be said and mimed in the right order each time. See how long a chain of actions you can call, without mistakes being made.

While the group repeats the chain of actions again, read out the memory verse to them, repeating it a couple of times if you wish, but the actions must continue all the time! Stop, and ask if anyone can repeat the verse to you? Now read the verse again, while everyone sits still and listens carefully.

Can anyone repeat the verse now? Repeat it aloud together, several times, until everyone can join in.

Theme points

As you can see, Martha was busy! Too busy to stop and listen to Jesus, like her sister Mary. The more you had to do, the harder it was to get the actions right. Why? Was it easy to remember the verse and do the actions as well? Why? Jesus said that Mary had chosen the right thing to do. There is nothing wrong with being busy and doing any of these jobs, but it's most important that when Jesus speaks we can be still, listen, and make time for him, and he will give us peace and strength.

41 Matching pairs

Themes

Loving one another, friendship

Bible link

John 15:12–17

You will need

Enough paper shapes for every child to have one – if there are an odd number of children, take one yourself to even the numbers. See diagram for how to cut the shapes – these are circles and squares cut in half, but no two have been cut the same way.

To play

Mix up all your paper pieces, and give one piece to every player. Explain that everyone has a few minutes to find their mystery friend. They can do this by trying to match their paper shapes with each other. Matched pairs should sit down together. See how quickly everyone can find their match and sit down. Shuffle the pieces and play again, if you wish, and see if you can match everyone any faster.

Theme points

We recognise our friends because we know them well. We usually know the kind of things they like to wear, and the things they like and dislike. What else is 'special' about a friend? We will help a friend in need, and we usually share their aims and interests. How can we be Jesus' friends?

42 Measure for measure

Theme

Giving

Bible link

Matthew 7:11,12; Luke 6:38

You will need

Container for each player – make these as varied as possible, eg eggcups, mugs, saucepans, yoghurt pots, jugs, jam jars, bowls. Fill one quite large container (a saucepan or jug) with water.

Mark the water level on the outside of the container.

To play

Game 1

Sit all the players round in a circle. Hand the jug of water to one player. Distribute the other containers at random, so that every player has one. Explain that on the word 'go', the player with the water will start to pour the water into the container of the player seated on their left. This player must pass the water to the player on their left, and so on around the circle. Some containers will only hold a small amount, they will have to keep refilling and pouring until the whole amount has been passed on. Care must be taken not to spill any – the aim is to end up with the original container refilled – with the same amount of water as at the beginning of the game! Check the level marker and see how successful you have been.

Now play again, with everyone swapping containers first, and see if you can do it any faster this time.

Game 2 – Team version

Play as before, but with the players seated in team lines. The last player in the line must run back to the beginning to pour the water into the original container. Award points to the fastest team, and to the team with the most water left at the end. For maximum effect, ensure that the last container in line is much smaller than the one at the beginning – lots of running and care will be required!

Theme points

Talk about giving and receiving. Note that all the containers were different, and some held more than others. We are all different, and have differing amounts available to give – not just of money, but of our time and talents too. This doesn't make any of us better or worse – it's the giving that counts.

43 Memory verse burst

Theme

Memory verses

You will need

Balloons – one per word for each set of verses, plus a few spares; small paper slips with the memory verse written on them – one word per slip, one complete verse for each team playing.

Roll the slips up, and insert each one into a balloon, blow it up, and tie the necks. Put two or three blank slips/balloons into each set for added fun! Keep the sets of balloons apart by putting each set into a bin liner.

To play

Divide your group into teams. If your group is small, the teams can be quite small; you could even play in pairs if you provide enough sets of balloons. There should be at least as many words in your verse as there are team members, so that in larger teams everyone can take part. Place the bin liners on one side of your playing space. Seat the teams together on the other side of your playing space.

On the word 'go', the team members take it in turns to run to the team's bin liner, grab a balloon, and pat it gently to keep it in the air back across to their team. Once there, they must stamp on the balloon to burst it and get the paper slip out. As soon as the paper has been retrieved, the next team member may run to get another balloon. Meanwhile, the remaining team members must begin to assemble their memory verse from the paper slips they have collected. The first team to reassemble a complete verse and sit down together with their hands up is the winner – let them shout their verse to you.

It may be helpful to have a leader holding each of the team bin liners so that it is easy for them to grab a balloon, and to prevent the whole lot coming out at once!

Theme points

Use this to focus on whatever theme or verse is appropriate to your session.

44 Mirror images

Themes

Actions, knowing Jesus, Bible heroes

Bible link

John 3:20,21; Romans 2:6–11

You will need

Strong supermarket fruit boxes, with the centres cut out to leave a narrow 'mirror' frame.

To play

Stand the mirror frames up on tables, weighing the bottom with books or similar objects, to stop them falling over during the game. Ask two children to come and sit or stand either side of the table, so that they can see each other 'framed' by the gap in the cardboard. If you haven't got frames, simply sit or stand the children in pairs, facing each other, about an arm's length apart. Explain that they are going to imagine that they are looking in a mirror. One player will start performing a set of actions, eg getting ready for school. This would involve hair brushing, teeth cleaning, clothes straightening, eating breakfast etc. The other must try to 'mirror' these actions as accurately as possible. The rest of the group can try to guess what they are doing. Then swap roles.

Children take it in turns to come forward and sit at the mirror. If necessary, give them ideas for miming, eg a new hairstyle, putting on a tie, trying on hats, putting on makeup etc.

For a particular themed link, eg with Bible heroes such as David or Samson, ask the paired children first of all to do mirror images of someone at work. This might be a vet, a policeman, a teacher. Present them for the group to guess 'who is in the frame?' Follow this up with your chosen hero in the frame – David killing Goliath with a slingshot, or dancing before the Lord, or Samson pushing the temple pillars down.

Theme points

Discuss afterwards how we recognise people by their actions. We know who they are, and what kind of person they are by what we see them doing. How can we recognise someone who follows Jesus? What kind of actions would we expect to see, and why?

45 More or less?

Theme

Giving

Bible link

Matthew 6:1–4; Mark 12:41–44; Luke 21:1–4

You will need

Dried peas, buttons or counters, disposable drinks cups or similar for each child.

To play

Give every child ten dried peas in a suitable small container. Explain that they are going to play a guessing game with each other. Show them how to play, by taking a few dried peas in your hand, without letting anyone see how many you have taken. Hold out your closed fist, containing the peas, and say to a volunteer, 'More or less?' The volunteer has to guess whether you are holding more or less than three peas, by calling out, 'More,' 'Less,' or 'Three.' If they are right, give them the peas. If they are wrong, they have to give you that number of their own peas. Now let them play the game with each other, taking it in turns to make the challenge, and moving on to another partner each time they have had a challenge and a guess with one partner. Let them play on for a few minutes, then call a halt while they all count their peas.

Theme points

Who has the most peas? How did they feel about giving away their peas? Was it easier to give a few away when you had lots of them? Why? How did you feel about giving peas away when you only had a few left? This is why Jesus praised the widow (Luke 21:1–4). You didn't know how many peas were in the other person's hand, you had to guess. Jesus says we should give to others secretly, too (Matthew 6:1–4).

46 None!

Themes

Sharing, serving

Bible link

Mark 9:35; Luke 9:46–48

You will need

Collection of 20 objects. The size of these objects will vary depending on the size of your playing area. For a tabletop game, these could be quite small objects like pencils, rubbers, small toy cars, toy bricks, small stuffed toys. For a floor game, try using larger objects like large cuddly toys, chairs, cushions, boxes. For a large group, try playing with 20 children in the middle, and for a pocket game, have twenty dried peas in a small container.

To play

Ask for two volunteers, and explain that they are going to play a game where they must take it in turns, as quickly as possible, to grab objects from the centre. They may choose to grab one, two or three objects each time – it's up to them, but the loser is the one who takes the last object. Onlookers can shout advice to the players, but keep it moving fast, giving a light-hearted cheer for the winner. Move on to a replay with another pair of volunteers, until everyone who wishes to has had a turn.

Team version

Divide the group into two teams, and allow them to choose together how many objects to grab each time. You may need to set a time limit for team discussions! Try counting down from 10 each turn.

Theme points

Talk about how easy/hard it was NOT to grab the last object. It took careful thought, and wasn't that easy. It can be like this in life – our instincts are to grab things for ourselves, but we have to learn how to share, how to serve one another and think of other people. Jesus tells us that 'the first shall be last and the last shall be first' which is a difficult idea in a world where winning is everything, and winning usually means having the most.

47 Pass it on!

Theme

Kindness to others

Bible link

Matthew 5:38–48; 7:11,12; Luke 6:27–31; Ephesians 4:25–32

To play

Seat all the players in a circle. Explain that you are going to pass actions around the circle. Any action may be chosen. The leader begins, by gently tapping the shoulder of the player on their left.

Everyone must, in turn, pass the action around the circle. When you are happy that they have got the idea, and nobody is hitting their neighbours (anyone who does this kind of thing must leave the circle for a turn or two) play on. Number players off round the circle, 1-2-3, 1-2-3, etc. Now explain that all the 1's must think of an action, and pass it to the left... now! There should be a wave of different actions going right around the circle. Then let the 2's, and then the 3's have a turn at starting the actions.

Suggested actions could be: rubbing noses, patting heads, tapping shoes together, slapping hands in a 'high five', shaking hands, hugging with one arm, tapping knees etc.

Theme points

Talk about how the actions returned. How do the things we do to others 'come back' to us? Good things and bad things come back in different ways. How might good things come back to us? How might bad things come back to us? How do we feel when we have done good/bad things to other people? What's the best way to live, in view of this?

48 Pennies in the pot

Themes

Giving, helping others

Bible link

Matthew 6:1–4; Mark 12:41–44; Luke 6:38; 21:1–4

You will need

Small coin or marble, clear playing space, wall or chair to represent 'home'.

To play

This game hinges on the fact that the group don't know who is going to be given the coin. Choose one player to start the game – he stands out in front of the group, holding the coin. The rest of the group stand in a row at one end of your playing space, opposite the 'home' wall or chair. They should hold their hands out, palms together, to make a 'pot' with their hands, leaving a small hole at the top. The player with the coin makes a similar 'pot', with the coin hidden inside. He walks along the line, placing his pot on top of the others in turn, secretly dropping the coin into any one of the other pots. The chosen player must not react at all at first. The original coin-holder must keep walking up and down the line pretending he still has the coin, until the chosen player decides to make a run for 'home', on the far side of the playing space. The other players now must try to tag him before he reaches 'home'. A successful runner becomes the new starter, but if he is tagged before reaching home, then the tagger becomes the next starter. (Starters cannot tag runners!)

Theme points

How did you know who to chase? It was hard, because the player with the coin dropped it in the pot secretly. Jesus tells us we should give to others secretly. Why? What will God do for those who give like this? (Matthew 6:1–4)

The coin was very small, but it was all you had. The poor widow only dropped two small coins in the temple treasury. Why did Jesus say that she had given far more than any of the rich men? (Luke 21:1–4) What does Jesus tell us will happen if we are generous to others, like this? (Luke 6:38)

49 Pillars of salt

Theme

Lot's wife

Bible link

Genesis 18:16 – 19:29

You will need

Music (live or recorded).

To play

Explain that when the music begins, everyone is to walk or dance around the room in the same direction in a circle. When the music stops, everyone must freeze exactly where they are. A volunteer then faces the wall. When the music stops, they turn round quickly, and look for the last person to freeze, or the first person to make a movement of any kind. That player must go and stand in the centre of the circle, frozen into a block of salt. They can choose to stand, sit, or crouch in any position they like, but once frozen, they must stay like that for the remainder of the game. The music restarts, and another round is played in the same way, with a second block of salt joining the first one in the centre. They can freeze in any position, but must touch the first block somehow. Play on, adding to your collection of frozen blocks, until everyone is frozen together in the centre of the room. The last remaining unfrozen player could become the leader for another round of the game.

Once they get the idea, children will enjoy finding silly poses to hold, and quite probably the whole pile of pillars will collapse before you finish – this doesn't matter at all, and adds to the fun. Simply start again, and encourage them to choose more stable poses next time round.

Theme points

The children were frozen into a pillar of salt if they made a wrong move in this game. Can anyone say what wrong move turned Lot's wife into a pillar of salt in the story? She disobeyed God by looking back at the destruction of the cities of the plain.

50 Praise balloons

Themes

Praise, celebration

Bible link

Exodus 15:1–21; 1 Chronicles 29:10–20; Luke 1:46–64; 2:13–20; 24:52,53; Acts 3:8,9; Ephesians 5:19,20; Philippians 4:4; Revelation 7:9–17

You will need

Inflated balloons (stored in an old duvet cover); indelible marker pens (OHP pens are ideal); lively music (live or recorded), whiteboard, clear playing space.

To play

Explain that you are going to have some fun praising God together. Ask the children what kind of things people say when they are happy and excited? Write some of these up where they can be seen. What words do people often use in church when they are praising God? Write these up as well. Your list might include: Hooray! Yes! Fantastic! Terrific! Praise the Lord! Now explain that you want everyone to choose ONE of these words or phrases, and copy it onto their balloon. Hand out the balloons, and if necessary, help them to write their chosen words. When everyone is ready, explain that you will play some music, and while it plays everyone must keep patting their balloon up in the air. Every time a player pats their balloon, they must shout the word they have chosen. Now play your music, and encourage everyone to leap about and keep their balloons in the air.

Top tip!

Have some spare balloons in case of bursting. Be ready to stop the music for lost balloons to be safely retrieved and rowdy players to calm down a little as necessary.

Theme points

David danced before the Lord. Miriam danced and sang. It's a great feeling to jump around and praise God with every part of your body!

51 Purse, bag, shoes 7-9

Theme

Apostles

Bible link

Matthew 10:5–15; Mark 6:7–13; Luke 9:1–6

You will need

For each team: purse or wallet, large holdall or rucksack, pair of adult-sized boots or trainers, piece of fruit, five or six chairs.

To play

Divide your group into teams of four or five, or play as one team together. Arrange a line of chairs down the length of your playing space, one line per team, with enough room for a child to weave in and out of the line. Pile a set of purses/bags/shoes at the far end of each team line.

The teams stand at the beginning of their line of chairs. On the word 'go', the first player from each team runs in and out of the line of chairs, grabs the purse from the team pile, and returns with it, in and out of the chair line, to the team. The next player is now free to do the same, fetching the bag, the third gets the fruit, followed by the fourth and fifth players in turn, fetching a boot each (or in a team of four, one player fetching both boots). When they have fetched all the equipment, one player must put on the boots, carry the bag, purse and fruit, and run back in and out of the chair line to the far side, closely followed by the rest of the team. The winning team is the first to be seated, with one fully equipped player, on the far side of your playing space.

Theme points

Was it easy running in and out of the chairs with a large bag and big boots? It was much easier without all the equipment. Why do you think Jesus told the disciples to take no bag, spare clothes, food, boots, sticks, gold or silver? All these things could slow them down in various ways – he wanted them to travel light, and to rely on God for their needs as they did his work.

52 Ring-on-a-string

This is a good calming-down game to play after a noisy one, and works well with all ages together.

Theme

Parables of the lost

Bible link

Matthew 18:12–14; Luke 15

You will need

Small plastic ring threaded onto a long length of string, joined to make a circle. The string needs to be long enough for the whole group, seated in a circle, to hold in both hands, with some space to slide their hands on the string. Keep the string pulled fairly tightly, to form a string circle linking the players.

To play

Practise sliding and passing the ring around the circle from hand to hand, without taking hands away from the string. Pass it backwards and forwards a few times to make sure everyone knows what to do.

One player conceals the ring under one of their hands. Now ask for a volunteer to step into the centre of the circle. This player must begin by closing his eyes and turning round three times, before trying to work out who has the ring. Meanwhile, the group must slide the ring around the string from hand to hand, and try to confuse the centre player so that he won't know who has the ring – fake passing adds to the fun. The players can chant, repeatedly, as they move their hands, 'Who's got the ring, the ring on the string?' The centre player shouts, 'Stop!' at any time he chooses, and taps the hand that he thinks conceals the ring. If he is right, the players exchange places, and play starts again from the beginning. If he is wrong, continue the game and give them two more guesses to find the ring before someone else has a turn in the middle.

Theme points

For a Bible link, such as with the lost coin, discuss how easy or hard it was to spot the ring. Is it always easy to find lost objects? Have the children ever lost something of value to them? Did they find it again? How did they feel when they realised their loss? How long did they search for it? How did they feel when they found it?

53 Rumble in the jungle

Themes

Guidance, safety

Bible link

Isaiah 30:21; Proverbs 29:25; Matthew 7:13,14

To play

Explain that everyone is to imagine that they are a troop of monkeys in the jungle. What kind of things do monkeys do? Encourage them to start acting like monkeys, then stop for a minute, and tell them that every troop of monkeys has a 'king', who warns them when danger, such as a hunter or predator, is coming. When the monkey king sees danger coming, he crouches down and puts his head down and his arms over his head – demonstrate this! They can all go and 'rumble in the jungle', but as soon as the monkey king crouches down, everyone must instantly do the same.

Explain that you will play the part of the monkey king for the first couple of times, and then others can take a turn. Now shout, 'rumble!' and join in the general havoc, crouching suddenly, without warning. When everyone is crouched down, shout 'rumble!' again, and play on.

Top tip!

For a final twist, try keeping the identity of the 'Monkey king' a secret each time, by secretly tapping your chosen king without the others knowing who you have chosen. This will really test their alertness, as they will have to try to watch every other player for the danger signal.

Theme points

Afterwards, ask them what kind of dangers God warns us about? How does he warn us, and how can we find safety?

54 Snakes in the grass

Themes

Snakes, temptation

Bible link

Genesis 3:1–13; Exodus 4:1–8; Numbers 21:6–9; John 3:14–17

You will need

Old sleeping bags or single-sized duvet covers, clear playing space, tape or chalk to mark a finishing line.

To play

Depending on how many sleeping bags/duvet covers you have available, play this with two or more children at a time. Choose two or three volunteers and give each child a sleeping bag. Explain that they are going to pretend to be snakes, and race each other across the room. The players get into their bags, and lie down, holding the bags closed at shoulder level, with their arms inside the bags. Line them up, and on the word 'go', they must wriggle and roll themselves to the other end of your playing space, completely crossing over the finishing line to win. The rest of the group can cheer them on, and everyone can have a turn.

For a team relay event, as soon as the snakes are clear of the finishing line, they can stand up and jump their way back to the beginning, get out of their bag, and hand it on to the next team member.

Top tip!

You will need to police this game to ensure every player remains flat on the floor and completely enclosed in their bags, and actually crosses the line before returning to the starting point. If you play the team version, try to ensure an even spread of ages and abilities between the teams. If any children find this too difficult – they need quite good coordination skills – step in and give them a judicious tug in the right direction!

Theme points

Where in the Bible do we first hear about a snake? Right at the beginning. How was the snake able to tempt Eve to eat the apple? By telling lies.

Most people instinctively recoil from snakes, however harmless some of them may be. We should instinctively recoil from temptation and lies. How can we recognise what is good and what is bad in our daily lives?

God turned Moses' stick into a snake, so that Moses could show that God was with him. (Exodus 4:1–8) Later, God told Moses to make a bronze snake on a pole, to heal those with snakebite who looked at it (Numbers 21:6–9), just as everyone who looks to Jesus is 'healed' of their sins and may have eternal life. (John 3:14–17)

55 Snip! Snap!

Theme

Love your neighbour

Bible link

Matthew 5:43–47; 19:19; 22:39; Mark 12:31; Luke 6:27–36; 10:25–37;
Romans 13:8–10; Galatians 5:14,15; James 2:8

To play

Two children at a time should come forward to play this. Make them
stand back to back, and explain that you are going to find out how well
they know one another. This works well with pairs of friends, but if your
group don't know one another that well, it doesn't really matter as
guessing the answers adds to the fun. Explain that you are going to ask
the first child a simple question; the answer will be either 'yes' or 'no'. The
first child must answer immediately, by turning a thumb up for 'yes',
down for 'no'. The second child must also give a thumbs up or down,
depending how they think the first child will answer. They must stay
standing back to back at all times, with no peeking allowed. Points are
awarded when the two of them are in agreement.

Questions could be, 'Have you got blue eyes?' 'Are you wearing
something red?' 'Do you like fish and chips?' Make the questions up as
you go along, and tailor them to the children playing. Keep the game
moving quickly, and change over after three or four questions to let the
second child answer the questions while the first guesses the responses,
then let another pair have a go.

Top tip!

This could be played as a team game, with pairs from each team
competing to score team points.

Theme points

The natural instinct was to respond to the question as though it was
asked of us, rather than our partners. It was an effort to keep thinking
about someone else all the time. We often find it hard to put others first,
and to care about them – Jesus tells us we should 'Love our neighbours'.

Getting to know each other is a step in the right direction!

56 Sounds right?

Themes

Choices, following Jesus

Bible link

John 10:1–16,27

You will need

Chair for every player (arrange them in a random pattern around the room, as far apart as possible, with enough space to allow children to pass between them), blindfolds, wrapped sweets or 'fun-size' packets of sweets, envelopes containing paper slips – for each round you will need two that say 'No!', and one that says 'Yes!'.

To play

Choose one volunteer to be blindfolded. Sit the rest of the children in the chairs. Explain that you are going to pick three children to call directions, but only one of these three will have a prize. Give three volunteers a sealed envelope, but do not open these yet! On 'go', all three envelope holders must shout directions to your blindfolded volunteer, who must try to find a way between the other seated children, to one of the shouters. When they have found one of the shouters, they must sit on their lap. Now the blindfold may be removed, and that envelope may be opened. If it says 'Yes!', then both children win a prize. If it says 'No', then nobody has won, and you should play again, with different volunteers, not forgetting to replace whichever envelope has been opened. In a small group, or with very young children, two callers may be enough.

Theme points

Play quite quickly, several times, and then pass sweets around to everyone in the group while you discuss what happened. How easy was it to find a caller? Fairly easy! How easy was it to find the RIGHT caller? Fairly hard! How do we decide who is telling us the right way to go, in life? What kind of things do people tell us to do? How do we decide which are good and which are bad choices? What can happen if we make wrong choices? Jesus tells us to follow his voice – to do as he tells us. Is this a good choice? Why?

57 Squeak!

Themes

Lost sheep, Jesus the good Shepherd, Peter, betrayal, Noah, hearing

Bible link

Genesis 6–10; Matthew 18:12–14; 26:69,70; Mark 14:66–68; Luke 15:1–7; 22:55–57; John 18:15

To play

Everyone sits down together, facing the front. One volunteer comes forward and stands with their back to the group. Unseen by the volunteer, the leader points to one member of the seated group, who must make a noise when the signal is given. The volunteer turns round as soon as the noise has been made, and tries to identify the noisemaker. If they are successful, the players exchange places, and play continues. If it proves difficult for the volunteer to spot the noisemaker, try having two or three noisemakers, to increase the chances of finding one. Change over after every three tries.

Theme points

Themed noises could be:

Baa! – The lost sheep, the Good Shepherd

Doodle-doo! – Peter's denial of Jesus, betrayal

Any animal noise the children choose to make – Noah.

58 Steering wheel

Themes

Listening, helping others, cooperation, following

Bible link

Matthew 4:19; 8:22; 9:9; 11:15; 13:9,43; Mark 2:14; 4:9,23; Luke 5:27; 8:8; 14:35

You will need

Blindfold for each team (use a scarf or an airline sleep mask), round tray or large paper plate for each team, simple obstacle course (use chairs, books, large cardboard boxes etc).

To play

This can be played by the whole group together, with members taking it in turns to be the 'driver', or play as a team race with teams competing to be the fastest through the course. Set up a simple obstacle course, shifting a few objects slightly when each volunteer driver has been blindfolded. Everyone lines up, single file, and holds onto the waist of the player in front of them. The player at the front of the line is the driver, and is blindfolded, and given a tea tray to use as a steering wheel. At the word 'go' the team must make their way through the obstacle course to the far side of your playing space – or right around the room – without bumping into anything. The driver goes first, with the rest of the team shouting instructions to them. If you have a large playing space and lots of children, two teams could race simultaneously, with double the amount of noise and confusion.

Theme points

This game actually works best if only one team member shouts instructions. Did anyone realise this? If everyone shouts, it gets very confusing. Life is the same. We have many 'voices' shouting to us: 'Buy this!' 'Wear that!' 'Go there!' 'Come here!' It can be hard to hear the voice of Jesus in all the noise we live in.

Other themes – helping one another, cooperation, following someone who knows where they are going.

59 Stormy weather

Themes

Jesus calms a storm, authority

Bible link

Matthew 8:23–27; Mark 4:35–41; Luke 8:22–25

You will need

Large sheet or blanket (or a play parachute if you have one), foam balls, tennis balls, beach balls, balls of screwed-up newspaper – as many as possible.

To play

Divide the group into two teams, with a minimum of four players per team. One team takes hold of the sheet – one player standing at each corner, the rest holding the sides as evenly as possible – and stretches the sheet out so it is taut. On the word 'go', the second team throw as many balls as possible into the centre of the sheet, while the first team must shake the sheet up and down as fast as they can, trying to make the balls fall off. The second team must run and fetch the balls, and throw them back onto the sheet as fast as they can. Let them play for a short time, then call out, 'Stop!' How many balls are there on the sheet? This is the score of the second team. Now swap over teams and play again, scoring as before. Repeat as often as you wish, or until they are unable to make waves any more!

In a very small group, play for fun, with four children taking turns to hold the sheet, and any others running about throwing the balls back on as fast as they can.

Top tip!

Initially, all the balls will be shaken off almost immediately. This doesn't matter – just keep the sheet stretched and the 'waves' going, and arms will soon tire enough to make scoring possible.

Theme points

Link with the story in Mark 4:35–41, where Jesus calms the storm. In your game, the 'storm' was calmed by a word from the leader. Why do the group obey the leader? In the story the storm was calmed by a word from Jesus. What does this show us about Jesus? Why were the disciples frightened?

60 Strange and wonderful

Theme

Creation

Bible link

Genesis 1

You will need

Large sheets of paper to pin up where everybody can see (the back of wallpaper rolls is ideal), felt-tip pens, scissors, glue, magazine pictures of 'strange and wonderful' creatures (optional).

To play

Explain that you are all going to create strange and wonderful new creatures! Give out large sheets of paper and ask them to draw, or cut out from the magazines and stick on, different parts of different creatures. For example, they might end up with an animal that has an elephant's ears, a kangaroo's body and a pig's tail. Set a time limit and at the end, stick all the creations up on the wall and judge which looks the most fantastic.

Theme points

Remind the children that God made everything in a marvellous way, and the world has many 'strange and wonderful' creatures in it – some of them far more strange and wonderful even than your pictures! At this point, you could show the group some pictures of exotic fish, insects or microscopic creatures, to illustrate this further.

61 Superstars

Theme

People in the Bible, Bible heroes

You will need

Clear playing space, masking tape or chalk to mark lines at either end of the space.

To play

This is a guessing game for the whole group to play together. One child (or a leader, to start the game) is chosen to be the 'caller', and goes to the far side of your playing space behind the line.

The rest of the children line up on the opposite side, behind their line. The caller thinks of a name – a 'superstar' of their choosing, such as a model, footballer, singer, or other famous person, and calls out their initials, eg 'DB' for David Beckham. The rest of the children try to think who this is. As soon as someone thinks they have the answer, they must run across, tag the caller, and run back behind their line to shout their answer. Answers may only be shouted out after running and from behind the start line. Any child may run at any time, the first to call the right name becomes the new caller. If a name is hard to guess, the caller may be asked for a category, eg sportsman, as a clue.

When everyone has grasped how the game works, announce a new category – people in the Bible, or Bible heroes – whatever fits your needs, eg JB – John the Baptist, A – Adam, Abraham, Andrew or Anna.

Theme points

Discuss the game afterwards. It started off as 'Superstars', then became 'God's superstars'. Discuss what made your Bible heroes so special.

62 Sweepers

Themes

Mary and Martha, listening to God, memory verses

Bible link

Isaiah 40:31; Luke 10:38–42

You will need

Broom, tennis balls and/or screwed up newspaper balls, bucket or box, memory verses.

To play

Seat your group in a wide circle, with enough space to move freely between the seated players. This is the 'house'. Don't explain the point of the game yet, but ask for a volunteer to be the first 'sweeper'. The sweeper is given a broom, and two or more tennis balls, depending on age and ability. (Younger children may find newspaper balls easier to control. Those who like a challenge may enjoy sweeping a mixture of the two!) Place the bucket or box on its side in the centre of the circle. The sweeper must sweep the balls, weaving in and out of the circle of seated players, until they have swept right around the house, keeping all the balls together as they go. Finally, all the balls must be swept into the box, and the sweeper can sit down again in the circle. Make sure that the sweeper has just enough difficulty controlling the number of balls to keep him concentrating hard on the job in hand, and going fairly slowly.

While the sweeper is cleaning the house, learn a memory verse together, eg Isaiah 40:31. Say this aloud, a word or two at a time, and get the seated children to repeat it with you, aiming to run through the whole verse together before the sweeper finishes. When the sweeper finishes, give them a round of applause, and ask them to repeat the memory verse. They will find it quite hard – ask why? Because they were concentrating on something else at the time – just like Martha! Now see if the rest of the group can repeat the verse? In theory, at least, they should remember it more easily than your sweeper!

Theme points

Ask who can tell you, now, why Jesus said that Mary had chosen the right thing. Play again, if you wish, with a different sweeper, and a different memory verse. Even though they know what to expect, it is still hard to listen and learn, and to concentrate on the job in hand at the same time.

What can we learn from this about our daily lives?

Alternatively, play this for fun, to help the group learn any memory verse you choose.

63 Tall stories

Themes

Bible stories, Bible quiz, mistakes, Noah

Bible link

Genesis 6–10

You will need

Rewritten Bible story, with lots of small deliberate mistakes, eg Noah: 'Once upon a time, there was a man called Noah. He had no sons, only daughters. God told Noah to build a helicopter. The animals went into the ark three at a time. It rained for a fortnight. The ark came to rest on top of a tree.'

Don't be afraid to put really silly things into the narrative. Once the children realise what is happening the children will listen all the more keenly to spot the mistakes. It may be helpful to use a highlighter to mark your 'mistakes' in your script.

To play

Game 1

Explain that you are going to tell them a story, but unfortunately things got a bit mixed up in your book, and you will need their help to sort it out. As you read the story to them, if they hear something that they think isn't quite right, they must put up their hands. Stop reading and ask them what was wrong. What should it be? Then carry on, in similar fashion, until you finish the story.

Top tip!

You could try playing this at the beginning of your session. Don't worry if they don't spot all the mistakes, but tell them afterwards how many mistakes they missed. Tell them they will hear it again at the end of your session, and see if they can spot all the mistakes second time around, by which time you will have gone over the 'proper' story as part of your session.

Game 2

Read the story 'straight' first time through, then tell the children that you will read it again, with a slight difference, to see how well they have remembered it.

Then read and play as in Game 1.

Theme points

Use any Bible story according to your needs.

64 Taste that!

Themes

Harvest, food

You will need

Pre-prepared mushy food samples in clean jars (take care to avoid allergy problems), clean lolly sticks, plastic spoons or similar for dipping and tasting, jug or bowl of hot water to dip and rinse between tastes.

Suggested food ideas:

Baby foods are ideal. Find simple single tastes if possible, eg pureed apricots, egg custard etc. If you use these, remove the labels from the jars.

Prepare your own by putting a small amount of mushy peas, apple puree, rice pudding, chocolate spread, fish paste, honey, jam, yeast spread etc into clean jars with lids.

Have water available to drink afterwards.

To play

Explain that at harvest time we celebrate all the good things that God has given to us, especially the food we eat. They are going to have some fun trying to work out what some of these foods are, just by tasting them!

If they don't want to try tasting things, they could try smelling them instead. Find pungent foods like curry sauce, mint sauce, oranges, chocolate spread etc, and cover the jars so that the contents can't be seen.

Either

Divide your group up into pairs. Let them take it in turns to taste from numbered jars, and write down what they think it is they've tasted. Let each pair try one taste at a time (no shouting out answers!). Then ask the whole group for their answers afterwards.

Or

Ask for volunteers to take it in turns to come forward and guess one jar at a time. If they get one wrong or can't guess, another person has a try.

Theme points

Not all the children will like all the flavours. Point out that we are all very different people, and we all have different likes/dislikes. God provides for everyone's tastes. Wouldn't it be boring if everything tasted exactly the same? Thank God for the variety of things he provides for us to eat.

65 Tell me

Themes

Families, children of God

Bible link

John 6:37; Romans 8:14–17; Galatians 3:26–29; 1 John 3:9,10

You will need

Whiteboard or large sheets of paper, list of categories, eg colours, fruit, animals, vegetables, birds, pop stars, flowers, food, countries, cars.

To play

Play either as a whole group activity, against the clock, or divide your group into two or more teams, and play the first part as a competition.

Begin by explaining that they will be given a category, and will have thirty seconds to think of as many items as possible that fit into it. Each team, in turn, is given a category, and when the clock starts ticking they all shout ideas for the leader to write up as fast as possible. Non-playing teams can be the 'clock', counting slowly aloud to thirty, or appoint a timekeeper for a slightly quieter version! At the end, announce one final category, 'Families', and ask the whole group to shout out as many ideas as they can. Who belongs in a family? Mum, dad, stepmum, foster brother, auntie... encourage the group to share as many ideas as possible. Finally, get a clean sheet of paper and write 'God's family' at the top. Who belongs in God's family? Let them think about this for a moment, then write EVERYONE across the page.

Theme points

Many children come from, or fear, broken families and relationships. Jesus has promised never to turn away anyone who comes to him – we can all feel secure in God's family.

66 Temptations

Themes

Temptation, sin

Bible link

Matthew 4:1–11; 6:13; 26:41; Mark 1:12,13; 14:38; Luke 3:2,3; 4:1–13; 11:4; 22:40,46

You will need

List of ideas for mimes, eg:

1 Being tempted to steal something.

2 Blaming someone else for breaking something.

3 Being unkind to an animal.

4 Being rude and answering back at school or home.

5 Copying someone else's work at school.

To play

Game 1 – Mime

Explain that you are going to think about what it means to be tempted to do wrong things, and how we might overcome temptation. Divide the children into small groups of three or four, and give each a situation to mime, or let them think up their own doing wrong/doing right mimes. Give them a few minutes to work out what they are going to mime, and then let them present their mimes in turn, with the rest of the group trying to guess what the subjects are.

Game 2 – Statues

Divide the group into two. Tell them that they are to imagine that the local council have decided to put up a statue in the town centre. It's going to be called 'Temptation' and there's a competition to see who can come up with the best idea! Now give the two groups a few minutes to pose and generally arrange themselves into a statue. Remember, statues don't laugh! Let them present their living sculptures to each other, with plenty of applause all round.

Theme points

Afterwards, discuss what you have just seen. Is it easy or hard to resist doing wrong things? What kind of things do we do that are wrong? What could we do instead? How do we feel after we have done wrong? How easy is it to do the right things? How do we feel then? What effects do our actions have on other people?

67 The name game

Themes

Starter game, God knows us all

Bible link

Psalm 139:16; 2 Timothy 2:19

You will need

Tennis ball, foam ball, beanbag or small soft toy to throw and catch.

To play

Everyone sits round in a circle; the leader starts the game by throwing the ball (or any suitable object) to another person in the circle. As the ball is thrown, the thrower shouts their own name.

The catcher throws the ball to someone else in the circle, shouting the first person's name AND their own name, each throw adding another name to the list. See how many times the ball can be thrown before a mistake is made. Once someone forgets the order, start play again with the last player going first for a new round. It doesn't matter if the ball is thrown twice to the same person – it's the sequence of names that's important. This works well with any number of players, including those who arrive while the game is in progress.

Top tip!

For a simpler game, or in a small group who know each other well, just shout your own name, and that of the person to whom you are throwing the ball.

Theme points

Use this to illustrate the point that God knows us all, whether we know him, or not. This would also make a good icebreaker game, helping a group to learn each other's names.

Variation

Use the same game to explore the following themes: New life, peace, forgiveness, happiness.

Bible link

Matthew 5:1–16; Luke 6:20–23; John 5:40; 8:12; 14:27; 16:33; 20:30,31

Theme points

Afterwards, discuss how you had to be ready to jump up at any moment to catch the ball. What sort of 'chances' do we get in life? (Making new friends, learning something new at school, going to see new places.) What sort of 'chances' does Jesus offer us? (New life, forgiveness, peace, happiness.) How can we grab the chances he offers us?

68 The peace game

A fun way of calming down over-excited children at any time.

Themes

Peace, following Jesus

Bible link

Isaiah 26:3; John 14:27; Philippians 4:6,7; Colossians 3:15

You will need

Large playing area.

To play

Everyone stands in front of the leader, or in a large circle with the leader in the centre.

Explain that everyone must copy the leader's actions instantly! The actions will flow rapidly from one to another, so they must watch carefully in order to keep up with the movements. The leader begins by performing some energetic actions, eg windmilling arms, miming driving fast, waving frantically – all the actions must be arm actions that flow into each other. Gradually, the pace of the actions slows down, the arms wave more slowly overhead, the fingers make waves and ripples, with the occasional slightly faster move thrown in, but overall the actions slow down. Now the leader makes the arms move slowly and sleepily up and down in calming movements, ending with the whole body and head dropping forwards and arms slack at the sides. If you wish, you could end with the whole body swaying gently and subsiding to the floor – invent your own movements until you are carrying everyone along with you.

Theme points

Sit down together in relaxed positions afterwards and discuss the game. How did they feel at the beginning? How did they feel at the end? What words can they give you to describe these feelings? Write them down if you wish. What is the best word for describing how you felt at the very end? Peaceful? Now discuss what Jesus means when he promises us his peace.

Use also as a game to illustrate the theme of 'following' someone by copying their actions.

69 The writing on the wall

Themes

Writing on the wall, humility, memory verses

Bible link

Daniel 5; James 4:10

You will need

Sheet of A4 paper for each word of your memory verse, Blu-tack or sticky tape, wall or suitable surface on which the words can be displayed, ball or beanbag, dartboard and darts.

To play

Game 1 – Whole group

For a game to link with Daniel 5, write the following verse onto your paper sheets, one word per sheet. Use a different coloured pen for each word, if you wish: 'Be humble in the Lord's presence, and he will honour you.' (James 4:10) Write chapter and verse on the final sheet to give you twelve sheets altogether. Shuffle these up, and pile them face down on the ground at one end of your playing space. At the opposite end, you should have Blu-tack and a flat display surface or wall.

Each person, in turn, runs to the dartboard and tries to score a total of at least 40 points with 3 darts. Only when they have scored 40 can they grab a word. They then run to the wall and stick the word up.

As more words are stuck to the wall, the rest of the team can start trying to put them into order – see how quickly they can stick all the words up AND get them in the right order.

Game 2 – Teams

For a team version, have two sets of words, two teams, and race to complete the unscrambled verse.

Top tip!

Provide a Bible at the end if they get completely stuck, so that someone can look up the correct order of words in the verse.

Position the dartboard slightly away from the rest of the people and make sure that one leader is stationed by the dartboard at all times to ensure safety. Remind the children playing never to run across in front of a dartboard during the game.

Theme points

Why did God send the writing on the wall? The clue is in Daniel 5:22. What was God telling the king? The clue is in James 4:10. Read this aloud from the wall together, taking away one word at a time, until you can say the whole verse unaided!

70 Travelling light

Themes

Travelling, guidance, people in the Bible

Bible link

Genesis 12,13; Exodus 13–19; Isaiah 30:21; John 14:6; Acts 13–28

You will need

Local maps, pens or pencils. For younger ages, try to find or draw simple maps of your local shopping centre etc. For older children, larger national maps are good fun but make sure your own area is featured.

To play

Game 1

Pin up two large-scale maps, and have two volunteers, with pens, who don't know where they are supposed to be going. Give them both the same starting point, marked on their maps. Divide the remaining children into two teams. Show them their team destinations on another copy of the map.

For maximum effect, give them different destinations approximately the same distance apart. Anyone who gives away the destination outright loses that game for their team! On your word to start, the teams must simultaneously shout directions to their volunteer, who must try to trace an accurate route to the team destination. Play for laughs, and have a replay with different players and destinations. Encourage cheering when destinations are successfully reached.

Game 2

Pin up two large-scale maps and tell the teams that you want them to find their way to a secret destination on the map. In order to do so, they must solve clues, one at a time, to find different destinations along the way. Give them the first clue. Clues might be picture clues, eg a picture of a crown for Queen's Street, or verbal ones. Only when they have solved the clue and found the place/street name it refers to, can they go to you for the next clue along the way. The winning team is the first one to reach the destination.

Theme points

Talk about the difficulty of finding your way in places you don't know, and about how it helps to have someone to help and guide you. Who guided Moses, Abraham and Paul? Who can guide us through life? What 'map' can we use? (a Bible). How can we find the way to God? See John 14:6 for a clue!

71 Treasure trove

Themes

Possessions, money

Bible link

Matthew 6:24–34; Luke 12:13–34; 16:13

You will need

List or magazine pictures (or actual objects) of twenty things that the children might like to own, pictures of a group of friends, the word 'Freedom'.

To play

Seat everyone in a circle. Show them the twenty items and tell them that if they were to be shipwrecked on a desert island, and could only have three of these things with them, which three would they choose? Move on through your pile of pictures, words and objects and find out who would take what, and why.

Theme points

When you have finished, ask which things you could do without. Go through them and vote again.

In theory, most people will vote to do without most things, but not friends and freedom.

How do we decide what is important in life, and what isn't?

72 Turn your back on it!

Themes

Temptation, sin

Bible link

Matthew 4:1–11; 6:13; 26:41; Mark 1:12,13; 14:38; Luke 3:2,3; 4:1–13; 11:4; 22:40,46

You will need

Set of lettered cards/pieces of paper, spelling RIGHT and WRONG – one set for each team; safety pins or sticky tape, empty matchbox for each team playing.

To play

Game 1 – Teams

You will need five children to stand up in front of the group for each team playing. On their backs, pin or tape the letters 'W-R-O-N-G' (one letter per child) and on their fronts, the letters 'R-I-G-H-T'. Make sure that the letters are paired correctly, so that when they all turn front or back, one complete word is visible. They begin the game standing with their backs to the group. The rest of the team (five or less) sit down in a row and play as follows. The child at the top of the seated row passes a matchbox to the next child in line, pushing it along the floor using only their nose. The matchbox is passed like this along the line to the end. The end child then picks the matchbox up, and runs to turn one of the letters round, then takes their place at the top of the team and passes the matchbox on again. Play is complete when all the letters are turned round. See which team is the fastest to turn from WRONG to RIGHT!

You could swap over the seated/lettered players and play a second round.

Game 2 – Whole group (less than 10 members)

Have five lettered volunteers, as before, and play for fun, with the rest of the group passing the matchbox and turning the letters as fast as they can. Change over for a second round and see if they can 'beat the clock' a second time round.

Theme points

What have you been doing in the game? Having fun turning WRONG into RIGHT! Does anyone know another word for wrong? The Bible calls it SIN. Luke has something to say about sin. Read aloud Luke 3:2,3. Is it easy or hard to resist doing wrong things? What kind of things do we do that are wrong? What could we do instead? How do we feel after we have done wrong things? How easy is it to do the right things? How do we feel then? What effects do our actions have on other people?

73 Up and away!

Themes

Holy Spirit, Pentecost

Bible link

John 3:7,8; Acts 2:2

You will need

Balloons, clear playing space.

To play

Give every player a balloon. Line everyone up to one side of your playing space. Let players come forward two or three at a time, blow up their balloons and hold them tightly to keep the air from escaping. At the leader's signal, they hold out their balloons and let them go. Mark where they land, and see whose balloon went the furthest. Play as many rounds as you wish.

For a team version, have competing players from each team releasing their balloons together, scoring points according to how far their balloons fly.

Theme points

How easy was it to control the distance flown by the balloons? It was practically impossible! We are told that it is like this with the Holy Spirit – we cannot predict where he will come from or where he will go next. We can't see the air in our balloons; we can't see the Holy Spirit. We can hear the noise that rushing air makes, and the people present on the day of Pentecost heard the sound of the coming of the Spirit 'like a mighty wind'.

74 Wacky races

Theme

Choices

Bible link

Proverbs 3:6

You will need

Fairly large playing area, 15 to 20 chairs, pre-prepared paper slips, in two categories, and two boxes or buckets to keep them in.

1. *Forfeits* Keep these very simple, eg, 'Sing a verse of a nursery rhyme,' 'Tell us a joke,''Whistle!''Stand on one leg and count to five without falling over,''Pat your head with one hand while rubbing your stomach with the other,''Count down backwards from 20 to 10.'Write these and/or others of your own onto slips of paper, fold in half, put in the bucket.

2. *Numbers* As many slips as you like, with numbers from one to six. Make sure there are a lot of threes and fours, and only one or two sixes. Slip in a few 'two backwards'. Place the chairs at intervals in a long line from 'Start' to 'Finish', or numbered sheets of paper taped up at suitable intervals. Alternatively, place the chairs in a wide circle, numbered round, with 'Start' and 'Finish' next to each other. (If you only have a small room, have the staging posts right around the perimeter, so that children are racing to travel right around the room.)

To play

The aim of the game is simply to travel right along the line of chairs and get to the finishing point as fast as possible. In order to do this, children have to make choices, which will have an effect on how soon they complete the race. They will take it in turns to choose from which bucket to take a slip. If they choose a forfeit, and successfully complete it, they can move up five places. If they refuse (or fail) to do the forfeit they will only move up one place. The numbers are a complete lucky dip from one to six, but beware of the 'two backwards'! Now let everyone take their turn. If two or more players arrive at one place at the same time, they all stand together at that point.

Keep the action moving fast. If anyone hesitates over a forfeit, just cry, 'Next!' and move them up a place before moving on – keep it light-hearted.

Theme points

Was it difficult to choose which bucket to pick? Were they all happy with their choices? Sometimes it's not easy making the right decision – we just have to do the best we can and we will get there in the end! What about choices we have to make in life? Choosing friends, games to play, foods to eat – how do we make these choices? How do we choose to follow Jesus/belong to him? What difference does this choice mean for us, and our lives?

75 Welly boot games

Themes

Abilities, disabilities, healing

Bible link

Acts 3:1–10

You will need

Two pairs of adult-sized Wellington boots (women's boots are best for smaller children; older ones will enjoy the challenge posed by men's boots!); whistle.

To play

Seat all the children on the floor in a large circle, with their shoes off. Place the boots in the centre of the circle. Choose two volunteers to start the game – preferably seated opposite each other. When you blow the whistle, they must run to the centre, pull on a pair of boots, run back through their places in the circle, round the outside of the circle and back to their starting places. The first child back and seated is the winner. Now play on, either with play passing one child to the left each time, so that everyone has a turn, or with new volunteers each time.

Extra!

You could play a similar game of 'Tag', with the chaser wearing the wellies – anyone tagged has to put the wellies on. Have two or three chasers in wellies, to even things out a bit!

Top tip!

Ensure that the boots aren't so big that they cause the children to fall.

Theme points

What was it like, trying to run in huge wellies? How did it feel to lose because you couldn't move properly? Discuss how it is like this all the time for a lame person. How would the lame person feel when they were suddenly able to walk and run properly? Play the game again, without the welly boots, if you wish, to illustrate the difference.

76 What a mess!

Themes

Mistakes, Jesus redeems

Bible link

Matthew 26:28

You will need

Game 1

Glacé cherries, washing-up bowls or large mixing bowls, water.

Game 2

Squirty cream, sweets – jelly sweets are ideal, trays, wet wipes or old towels for cleaning up afterwards.

To play

Game 1

Fill the bowls with enough water to make retrieving the cherries interestingly difficult but not impossible. (Generally speaking, the older the children, the deeper the water!) Adjust to suit individual players as necessary. (Make sure you have adequate adult supervision.)

Drop a cherry into each bowl. Explain that you want a volunteer to come and try to grab the cherry, using only their teeth – hands must be clasped behind backs. Time them, and see who can be the fastest to grab a cherry.

Game 2

Squirt a mountain of cream onto the middle of the tray. Place a sweet in the centre of the top of the cream. Explain that you want a volunteer to come and try to grab the sweet, using only their teeth – hands must be clasped behind backs. Time them, and see who can be the fastest to grab a sweet.

Team version

Have two trays, and run it as a team competition, with team members in turn coming forward to grab a sweet or cherry. Replace the sweet after each turn, and see which team finishes first/fastest.

Top tip!

Explain first and then squirt the cream – it disintegrates quite quickly.

Theme points

Everyone got into a real mess in this game. Sometimes we make a real mess of our lives. We fall out with friends, we get into trouble at school etc. Jesus has promised to help us to wipe out our mistakes and help us start again.

77 What did you say?

Theme

God knows us all

Bible link

Psalm 139:4

You will need

Pre-prepared slips of paper with simple words written clearly on them, eg cat, egg, table, foot, bed, car etc.

For a specific, seasonally appropriate game, play with random words to begin with, and then end with your particular word eg Easter, Christmas, Harvest or Pentecost, and see what connections the children can make.

To play

Game 1 – Whole group

Explain that when people say a word, we sometimes think of 'associated words'. For example, if you say 'cup', I might think of 'saucer', or 'tea', or 'coffee' – these are words we readily put together in our minds. In this game, players will see just how often they can guess what words will come into each other's minds in this way.

Choose a volunteer to leave the room for a minute. Make sure that the volunteer can't hear your discussion. Show the remaining children one of the word slips, eg 'egg'. Now they must decide what they think that the volunteer will say, when they come back and is shown this slip. Encourage the group to share ideas quickly, eg 'boiled', 'Easter', 'chicken'.

Have a quick vote by show of hands for the most popular response, then invite the volunteer back in again. Show them the word and see what they say. Were the group right or wrong? Keep a score, and find out how many times the group gets it right. Keep the game moving as fast as possible, with a new volunteer leaving the room each time until everyone's had a turn.

Game 2 – Team version

Play as before, but with the group in two teams, and a volunteer from each leaving the room. The teams choose their own answers, with each team being given a different word each time. Teams should guess their volunteer's response, and score a point for a right answer.

Top tip!

Emphasise that it does not matter if they get the right answer or not – the fun is in guessing what people will say.

Theme points

The Bible says, 'Before I even speak a word, you know what I will say.' (Psalm 139:4) We did our best in this game to guess what others would say. God doesn't have to guess – he knows us so well, he knows how we will react and what will say, anytime, any place, any day!

78 What's that?

Themes

Noah, creation, Harvest, Christmas

You will need

Play dough or similar, plastic sheeting/tablecloth for work surface.

To play

Noah – tell the children to each make a model animal, but not to tell anyone what it is. After a set time, they take it in turns to display/guess the animals (with or without sound effects!).

Creation – tell the children to model something God has made, either from the Bible story, or their own ideas.

Alternatively

Play as a team relay, or individually in turns. The children come forward, model an animal or other item from a list held by the leader, which the teams or whole group must identify. See how fast they can go – how many animals can be modelled and identified in 5 minutes?

Seasonal variations

Play as for the Noah game, but substitute related seasonal objects for the animals, eg:

Christmas – stars, angels, manger, shepherd, sheep, wise man, gift, donkey, stable. If you keep all the models, bake, paint and put them together – at the end you will have made your own crib set!

Harvest – model fruits and vegetables. If you keep these, they could be baked and painted as a follow-on activity after the game.

Theme points

This is a fun way of starting discussion about your chosen Bible story.

79 Who are you?

Themes

Love your neighbour, Good Samaritan

Bible link

Matthew 5:43–48; Luke 6:27–36; 10:25–37

You will need

Blindfold.

To play

Everyone sits in a circle. One volunteer (also seated in the circle) is blindfolded, and calls 'Change!' This is the signal for everyone else to change places with each other, at random.

When everyone is seated again, the blindfolded player says, 'Who are you? Give me a clue!' holding a hand out to their left or right. The player seated on that side takes hold of their hand and says 'Help!' a couple of times, before letting go. The blindfolded player tries to guess the identity of the speaker. If they guess wrongly, then they repeat the words and actions with the child seated the other side. If both guesses are wrong, 'Change!' is called again, and play continues. A correct guess means the speaker is blindfolded in turn, and the original volunteer rejoins the group.

Change blindfolded volunteers after two rounds if they can't identify anyone – keep the game moving quickly.

Theme points

How easy was it to recognise your 'neighbour'? Some were easier than others. What is a neighbour? Someone near or next to you. Some neighbours we know better than others, and some we sometimes don't want to know. What did Jesus tell us about our neighbours?

80 Who do you think this is?

Theme

Who is Jesus?

Bible link

Luke 9:18–20,35

You will need

Paper, pens.

To play

Game 1

Give everyone (leaders as well) a slip of paper. Everyone must write down three things about themselves. These could be their favourite food, TV programme, a famous person they admire, etc. However, one of these things must be untrue. Be ready to help younger or less able children if needed. Get each person to read their three 'facts' and get the rest of the group to vote on which they think are true and which is not.

Game 2

If everybody there knows each other, do the same as above but fold the papers so nobody else can see, and shake them together in a bag. Invite different children to take one at random, read them aloud, and see how many they can match to the authors. Play this quickly – don't linger trying to guess the harder ones – and there is no need to do all of them if time is short.

Theme points

Some facts about people were easier to identify than others – which were the easiest? Probably the people who talk a lot because we know more about them. Quiet people can be harder to guess at! Some people find it easier to see who Jesus really is than others. How can we 'see' Jesus around us today? We should be able to see Jesus in the lives and work of Christians around us – what kind of things might we expect to see Christians doing?

81 Whose feet?

Theme

Who is Jesus?

Bible link

Luke 9:18–20,35

You will need

Old sheet or curtain.

To play

Hang the sheet or curtain over a suitable doorway, so that only the feet and ankles of someone standing outside are visible. Divide the group into two (or more) teams. One team goes to the other side of the curtain, out of sight, and takes off their shoes and socks, rolling up their trouser legs, leggings etc. They then take it in turns to parade past the doorway with only their feet and ankles visible.

The other team then tries to guess 'Whose feet?' Keep it moving fast. There should be no personal comments allowed! It adds to the fun if leaders also participate.

Change over, so that everyone has a turn at parading their feet and guessing their owner's identity.

Theme points

Point out that we are all different people, with a unique identity and characteristics of our own. Jesus is a unique person too – his actions show this clearly. What is it that makes Jesus different? He's God's Son.

82 Who wants to have fun?

Theme

Bible quiz

You will need

List of pre-prepared quiz questions each with four possible answers
(base these on the topic/Bible passage of your choice), three sheets of
paper with the following words written clearly on one side: '50/50' 'Ask a
friend' 'Ask the team', large sheet of paper or whiteboard with this
written on:

(1) 100
(2) 500
(3) 1,000
(4) 5,000
(5) 10,000
(6) 50,000
(7) 100,000
(8) 1,000,000 points!

To play

This is ideally played as a team game, with two teams, each team
choosing a volunteer to play 'Who wants to have fun?'

The volunteer comes forward, and you explain that they have a great
opportunity to win a million points for their team! All they have to do is
answer eight questions correctly. Show them the pyramid scale. The first
question is worth 100, the second 500, and so on, up to a million points.
Now show them the sheets of paper. These are the 'lifelines'. If they can't
answer a question, they can choose to use a lifeline. 50/50 means that
you will eliminate two wrong answers. Ask a friend means that they can
ask a friend for the answer. Ask the team means they can ask their team
for the answer. They can only be used once each!

Hand the sheets to the volunteer, to be handed back as they are used.
Play the game by asking the multiple-choice questions. Each time a
correct answer is given, put a team mark (use a different colour for each
team) against the score achieved so far. Lifelines may be used whenever
the player wishes to do so, but players must beware – any wrong
answers mean they lose ALL their points!

They can choose to stop playing at any time, if they don't know the right answer, and their team will keep all the points scored. Keep a running total of team scores, and alternate play between teams.

Top tip!

Make the first few questions as easy as possible, and pitch them to the age and ability of the players.

Keep some really difficult questions in hand so that winning a million isn't easy – anticipation is what keeps this game going!

Why not have a weekly play-off of two rounds of this game, based on your Bible story of the week? Keep a monthly score of the grand totals, and see which team can have the most fun!

Alternatively, play as a whole-group activity, with children taking it in turns to be in the hot seat, or let them play in pairs, helping each other to decide on their answer.

Theme points

Use this game as a fun way of encouraging children to think about what they have learned.

83 Zip! Zap!

This is a fun game to play at the beginning of a session while people are still arriving. Use as a game to open discussion of how we often copy what other people are doing, without really thinking about where our actions will lead us.

Themes

Starter game, relationships

To play

Everyone sits round in a circle, and holds their hands in front of them, palms together, fingers pointing to the centre of the circle. One player starts off, by wagging their hands to left or right. If they wag to the left, they must shout, 'ZIP!' If they wag to the right they must shout, 'ZAP!' The person immediately to their left/right must respond immediately likewise, wagging their hands either left or right, and shouting, 'ZIP!' or,

'ZAP!' as appropriate. When the players are familiar with this, add ZOOM! as an alternative action – hands may point across the circle to any other player, who then picks up and carries on the actions. Finally, add BAM! If anyone is sent a ZOOM! they can say BAM! and send it right back to the sender.

Top tip!

For extra fun, with a big group, or with an especially competent one, try introducing a second wave of zip-zaps, to run at the same time as the original one.

Theme points

Some children will develop mini-trials of strength with each other, zip-zapping and zoom-bamming back and forth between the two! Use this as a way of initiating discussion of why we do this sort of thing. Why do some people refuse to give way to each other? What sort of effects do these kinds of actions have in real life situations?

You may like to add a rule that actions may only be bounced three times, if this blocks the game.

Theme index

Bible index